J.R.R. TOLKIEN

A BEGINNER'S GUIDE

ANDREW BLAKE

Series Editors
Rob Abbott & Charlie Bell

Hodder & Stoughton

A MEMBER OF THE HODDER HEADLINE GROUP

Orders: please contact Bookpoint Ltd, 130 Milton Park, Abingdon, Oxon OX14 4SB.
Telephone: (44) 01235 827720, Fax: (44) 01235 400454. Lines are open from 9.00–6.00,
Monday to Saturday, with a 24-hour message answering service.
You can also order through our website www.madaboutbooks.co.uk

British Library Cataloguing in Publication Data
A catalogue record for this title is available from The British Library

ISBN 0 340 85797 8

First published 2002
Impression number   10 9 8 7 6 5 4 3 2 1
Year 2007 2006 2005 2004 2003 2002

Cover photo from Hulton Archive
Typeset by Transet Limited, Coventry, England.
Printed in Great Britain for Hodder & Stoughton Educational, a division of Hodder Headline

CONTENTS

How to use this book

The *Beginner's Guide* series aims to introduce readers to major writers of the past 500 years. It is assumed that readers will begin with little or no knowledge and will want to go on to explore the subject in other ways.

BEGIN READING THE AUTHOR

This book is a companion guide to Tolkien's major works, it is not a substitute for reading the books themselves. It would be useful if you read some of the works in parallel, so that you can put theory into practice. This book is divided into sections. After considering how to approach the author's work and a brief biography, we go on to explore some of Tolkien's main writings and themes before examining some critical approaches to the author. The survey finishes with suggestions for further reading and possible areas of further study.

HOW TO APPROACH UNFAMILIAR OR DIFFICULT TEXTS

Coming across a new writer may seem daunting, but do not be put off. The trick is to persevere. Much good writing is multi-layered and complex. It is precisely this diversity and complexity which makes literature rewarding and exhilarating.

Literary work often needs to be read more than once and in different ways. These ways can include: a leisurely and superficial reading to get the main ideas and narrative; a slower more detailed reading focusing on the nuances of the text and on what appear to be key passages; and reading in a random way, moving back and forth through the text to examine different aspects, such as themes, narrative or characterization.

In complex texts it may be necessary to read in short chunks. When it comes to tackling difficult words or concepts it is often enough to guess in context on the first reading, making a more detailed study using a dictionary or book of critical concepts on later reading. If you prefer to look up unusual words as you go along, be careful that you do not disrupt the flow of the text and your concentration.

VOCABULARY

You will see that keywords and unfamiliar terms are set in **bold** text. These words are also defined and explained in the glossary to be found at the back of the book.

This book is a tool to help you appreciate a key figure in literature. We hope you enjoy reading it and find it useful.

✳ ✳ ✳ *SUMMARY* ✳ ✳ ✳

To maximize the use of this book:

- read the author's work;

- read it several times in different ways;

- be open to innovative or unusual forms of writing;

- persevere.

Why read J.R.R. Tolkien?

Tolkien is one of the most popular twentieth-century writers, and this book tries to help explain that success – which is, on the face of it, very surprising. Here is an author who spent his professional life in a university department, teaching works of literature written in languages no longer spoken, and publishing a few learned essays. He had a very quiet life – a family and a small circle of friends. He enjoyed talking, and walking in the countryside; he didn't travel widely. Then in middle age he published *The Hobbit*, a children's book in which a character of his own invention, a hobbit, goes off for an adventure with a wizard and a group of dwarves – on the way they encounter trolls, a dragon, goblins and elves. The publisher asked for a sequel, but instead Tolkien wrote a very long book for adults, published in three volumes, which echoed many of the mythologies of the old cultures he taught. The characters in this book use words from the languages he invented, they keep reciting poems, there is plenty of violent adventure but very little romance and absolutely no sex, and the principal characters defeat a great evil, but destroy the world they are living in. This is hardly a normal formula for literary success.

On publication this book, *The Lord of the Rings*, was poorly received by the critics – but it sold well, and after fifteen years or so of 'cult' status a publishing dispute in the USA helped it to become one of the most successful of all twentieth-century novels. If, that is, you can call it a 'novel'. Meanwhile Tolkien's work entered popular culture – it has generated a parody (*Bored of the Rings*, which is also a best seller), and a number of computer games. In the early twenty-first century *The Lord of the Rings* was made into a Hollywood hit movie.

This an amazing story – though perhaps more amazing is that *The Lord of the Rings* has consistently been voted the greatest twentieth-century novel in English, comfortably outpacing rivals such as James Joyce's *Ulysses* and Salman Rushdie's *Midnight's Children* (each of which is more popular with the critics). But there is more to Tolkien than *The Lord of the Rings*, and this book will examine how all his other writing contributed to the success of his best-known work.

Tolkien did not write much for publication. Apart from *The Hobbit*, *The Lord of the Rings*, and a number of academic essays, only a few short stories and poems were published during his lifetime. However, Tolkien's friends and family knew that behind these stories was a lifelong project. He invented languages in fine detail, and he created myths and legends to accompany them. After Tolkien's death it became clear that there were a great many supporting works which told what happened before *The Hobbit* and *The Lord of the Rings*, and many of these papers have been edited and published by Tolkien's son Christopher.

These supporting works recount those different languages, and explain how they developed. They tell and retell the stories of the 'races' which have inhabited his imaginary world, Middle-earth as Tolkien calls it: the elves and dwarves, goblins (or 'orcs'), wizards and dragons, the tree-herding ents, the hobbits, and the men. The stories of these very different thinking creatures who have lived on Middle-earth give a number of different perspectives on its history and development. Because he had worked on these stories throughout his life, Tolkien was able to give *The Lord of the Rings* an amazing sense of depth – its history, mythology and poetic traditions are richer than anything in the old poems such as *Beowulf*, which were among his sources, or the other fantasy writers who have tried to copy Tolkien. We read Tolkien because, in this way, he makes fantasy seem real.

The most important of the posthumous works, *The Silmarillion*, appeared soon after Tolkien's death. It is a long and complex book, which starts with the founding of a world, and explores the problems of good and evil, and of bravery and creativity in that world. Although

The Silmarillion has never become as popular as *The Lord of the Rings*, as it is deemed to be difficult to read, the themes give you some idea why his other work is so popular. As well as establishing a fantasy world which is very 'real' due to the detailed work he put in on its component parts, Tolkien puts the apparatus of language, character and plot to good use by exploring these universal themes – asking who made the world, who or what has responsibility for it, and why there is evil and pain. Even in a world which seems increasingly less inclined to religious belief, these remain very important issues. Too few contemporary writers face them. The light realist comedy of Nick Hornby, the elegant romanticism of Anita Brookner, or the darker imaginings of Ian McEwan, all have something to offer the reader who wants to decode the modern world. But they do not have much to say about the bigger issues. Tolkien may not have the answers, but he asks the questions – and many of us want to stand alongside him as he looks at the world, asks, and wonders.

❋ ❋ ❋ *SUMMARY* ❋ ❋ ❋

While Tolkien's stories are exciting adventures, he is also an author who deals with big issues. His writing helps us to think about:

- how we define 'good' literature – and who does the defining.

- ways in which new writing can draw upon older forms.

- ways in which literature deals with 'the big issues' such as good and bad, and life and death.

2 Approaching Tolkien's Work

WHERE SHOULD I BEGIN?

The Lord of the Rings is set in Middle-earth, a world like ours, with its own languages, peoples and histories. The action takes place thousands of years after Middle-earth was first populated. *The Silmarillion* offers us much of the rest of that story, from the creation of the world onwards, and it might seem appropriate to start here, but very few people do. The most rewarding place to start reading and appreciating Tolkien's work is with *The Lord of the Rings*. It can be read firstly as an exciting adventure story in which good eventually conquers evil. *The Lord of the Rings*, partly due to its length, invites re-reading, and those who read it again usually find that they are beginning to explore the book's more complex ideas – love, duty, sacrifice, cultural difference, and the importance of attempting to preserve a way of life, to name but a few. Many readers then go on to explore the rest of Tolkien's work.

The Lord of the Rings may appear a little daunting at first sight. It is very long, and it is written in slightly unfamiliar English. Many of the characters quote verse at each other rather than have conversations, and when they do talk they often use stilted, old-fashioned and very formal language. Furthermore some of the poetry quoted in the text is in languages of Tolkien's own invention. The first-time reader needs to develop a sympathy for this unusual writing style, and most do so quickly and easily.

The reader quickly recognizes that the imagined languages have the ring of truth about them. As a professor of Anglo-Saxon, Tolkien taught languages such as Old English and Icelandic, and when he wasn't teaching he was inventing languages based on classical Greek, Welsh and Finnish as well as Anglo-Saxon and the Scandinavian languages. Having produced grammars and vocabularies, Tolkien invented the various mythologies, histories and geographies of Middle-earth, in order to provide some background for the languages – the stories came out of this background, and not the other way round. In the case of *The Hobbit*, the story – written for children – lies very much on the surface, with few traces of that complex 'past', which he had invented. *The Lord of the Rings* makes far more detailed references to the other peoples, times and events of Middle-earth, and it has a set of scholarly appendices which give the reader a flavour of the author's project as a whole.

The Hobbit and *The Lord of the Rings* are out of the ordinary, but they are comparatively straightforward exercises in storytelling. The style and form of Tolkien's other long works are indeed unusual. Most of these – *The Silmarillion* and the collected *Unfinished Tales* and other material which has been published since Tolkien's death – are written as if they are either myths, or political histories of a world very like our own, with echoes of historical documents such as the *Anglo-Saxon Chronicles*. They tell of events and changes in the governing of the world, and of the most important characters in those events – but they don't portray the characters' thoughts or desires in any detail, in the way you would expect from a novel by Dickens, say. So it is very difficult to read them as 'novels', and although they depict action which takes place before the start of *The Hobbit* and *The Lord of the Rings*, these works make more sense, and they are easier to read, if you have read *The Lord of the Rings* first.

But if they are not novels, what are all these myths and histories about the first two Ages of Middle-earth? Are they simply a form of intellectual hobby to help a clever Oxford don while away the time? The author himself tended to support this idea. He referred to his language-making activities in a published lecture as a 'secret vice'. It's easy to dismiss this as a typical piece of English understatement, but Tolkien insisted that his work was not topical. In other words, although most of it was written during the Second World War, and it describes a war against the forces of evil, *The Lord of the Rings* is not meant to be about the fight against the Nazis, or the use of the first nuclear weapons. This may be true – there is no exact parallel between Hitler and Sauron, or between the rings of power and the Hiroshima bomb – but in saying so Tolkien tended to dismiss the wider meaning of his writings.

The Lord of the Rings remains the obvious starting point for readers, and everyone interested in Tolkien should read it. But if you don't think you are ready to start exploring the unfolding history of Middle-earth there are several much shorter pieces of writing in a more accessible style, which will introduce you to Tolkien's art and ideas without exposing you to the tangled weave of Middle-earth's languages and histories. Each features ordinary men who are chosen by fate to do something special (a key theme in *The Lord of the Rings*). *Smith of Wootton Major,* for example, tells of a human encounter with the enchanted world, and stresses the importance of giving up power and handing it on to the right people. *Farmer Giles of Ham* is about a cheery man who defeats a giant and a dragon, puts the King and his knights to shame, and establishes a kingdom of his own. *Leaf by Niggle* explores the ways in which art and community should fit together through the portrayal of a man reflecting on his skills as a painter and his shortcomings as a neighbour while he journeys towards his own death. His painting becomes a gateway to heaven. There is something of Tolkien himself in all three of these characters, and reading these stories will help to prepare you for the wider canvas of the longer works.

✳ ✳ ✳*SUMMARY*✳ ✳ ✳

- Read *The Lord of the Rings* before tackling *The Silmarillion* and the other long works.

- If *The Lord of the Rings* looks daunting, don't start with *The Hobbit* – read *Smith of Wootton Major, Farmer Giles of Ham,* and *Leaf by Niggle,* then *The Lord of the Rings.*

- These are complex works, and you will get more out of all of them by reading them several times.

Tolkien's Life, Work and Legacy 3

AN UNEVENTFUL LIFE

The authors' life story can be told very briefly. John Ronald Reuel Tolkien was born in 1892 in Bloemfontein, South Africa, which was at that time part of the British Empire. Three years later his father died, and the family – a mother and two sons – moved to a country cottage on the outskirts of Birmingham. Tolkien's mother died in 1903, and the young orphans were looked after by a Catholic priest. Tolkien went to school in Birmingham, then to Oxford University. After military service in the First World War (1914–18) Tolkien married Edith Bratt, also an orphan, whom he had known since he was sixteen. They subsequently had three sons and a daughter. Tolkien worked for a while on the *Oxford English Dictionary*, a huge undertaking which was nearly finished by the time he worked on it – he wrote some of the 'W' entries. He then became Professor of English Language and Medieval Literature at Leeds University, and in 1925 he was appointed Professor of Anglo-Saxon at Oxford University. Tolkien remained at Oxford for the rest of his professional life. He retired in 1959, and during his retirement stayed mainly in Oxford (there were also a few years in the seaside town of Bournemouth before Edith died in 1969). J.R.R. Tolkien died in 1973.

By the time he died, Tolkien had become a world-famous author. *The Hobbit* was published in 1937. It was successful enough for publishers Allen and Unwin to ask for a sequel. Eventually the three volumes of *The Lord of the Rings* appeared in 1954 and 1955. In the 1960s, publicity following a dispute over an illegal American edition of *The Lord of the Rings* helped to boost sales of the trilogy, and a 'cult' success became a global best seller. A few shorter pieces such as the poetry collection *The Adventures of Tom Bombadil* and the short story *Smith of Wootton Major* were published during the 1960s, but despite public demand there was no sequel to *The Lord of the Rings*. Since Tolkien's death a great deal more material about Middle-earth and its history has become available. *The Silmarillion* finally appeared in 1977, in a version edited by Tolkien's son Christopher, who went on to edit a number of his father's other writings on Middle-earth, commencing with *Unfinished Tales* in 1980. Since then, Christopher has laboured to produce a definitive account of the evolution of his father's imaginative writings and imagined languages – for a while these were collected in a five-volume sequence of *Lost Tales*, but this has been replaced by a twelve-volume *History of Middle-Earth*, which includes those unfinished tales and a great deal more.

PHILOLOGY – TOLKIEN'S PROFESSION

Tolkien was a professional philologist. **Philology** is an old-fashioned term nowadays; most people involved in the academic study of language call what they do **linguistics**. Tolkien was not just interested in language and meaning, but in the historical development of the languages of Britain and northern Europe, and in the literature which was written in those languages. Most of his teaching was of Old English (or Anglo-Saxon) and Middle English (the language of Chaucer).

Early in his career he co-edited a scholarly edition of the Middle English poem *Sir Gawain and the Green Knight* (he subsequently translated the poem into modern English, and the translation was published along with two others, *Pearl* and *Sir Orfeo*, after his death).

KEYWORDS

Philology: literally 'the love of words'. Philologists study the ways languages evolve, which often means using literature as evidence of historical changes in languages.

Linguistics: the term usually used now for the scientific study of languages. Professional linguistics is less interested in the historical evolution of languages than in what they mean now, and it uses speech for evidence rather than literature.

Probably his most important academic publication was the essay 'The Monsters and the Critics'. Here Tolkien discusses the Old English poem *Beowulf* – in which a heroic individual defeats several monsters, in the end at the cost of his own life. Tolkien defended the poem as a great work of art against those critics who simply used it to help teach or study the evolution of the English language. This essay, like the edition of *Sir Gawain*, is still in use in English courses today. Though his academic output was slight (he was a perfectionist, lacking in self-confidence, who refused to publish anything he did not think was complete), Tolkien's influence was and still remains important.

TOLKIEN'S LITERARY INFLUENCES

Beowulf, Sir Gawain and the Green Knight and the other Arthurian stories; the *Mabinogion* and other Welsh legends; and the stories of the Norse gods and heroes as told through the Icelandic *Sagas*, formed the deep background for Tolkien's own stories, while the languages that these tales were written in (and also Finnish, classical Greek, and Gothic, a Germanic language) are among the inspiration for his own invented languages. None was more important to him than the Finnish language, and the Finnish national epic poem, the *Kalevala*. This long poem was compiled during the nineteenth century by a scholar called Elias Lönnrot, who deliberately made a national mythology from the old poems and stories in Finnish which survived from the pre-Christian era. Tolkien was fascinated by the rolling syllables of Finnish, and by the poem's tragic, and heroic, content.

Tolkien began to invent similar languages of his own, and to write poems in them. He realized that there was no equivalent in English literature to the *Kalevala*. While Britain was the centre for the Arthurian tales, including *Sir Gawain*, most of the medieval Arthurian stories were written in French, and in any case they were about Celtic British, not English, heroes. The few surviving heroic poems in Old English were unsuitable for a national mythology – *Beowulf*, for example, is about Scandinavian heroes, while *The Battle of Maldon* is about the defeat of Anglo-Saxons by the invading Vikings. As Tolkien saw it there was no 'mythology for England', and he, and friends such as C. S. Lewis and the poet and novelist Charles Williams, tried to provide one.

So Tolkien invented languages which were rather like Finnish, Welsh and Anglo-Saxon, and provided a mythical world of his own in which people actually spoke them. In order to do so he turned to the existing literature of fantasy and tried to draw up a set of rules for his own use. One of Tolkien's few published essays is a transcript of a talk he had given, 'On Fairy Stories'. This essay defends fantasy literature as an adult genre, against the tendency (which is already visible in Shakespeare's *Midsummer Night's Dream*) to reduce the fairy world (or Faërie as he calls it) to harmless little people in amusing stories for children. Tolkien was familiar with the fairy stories and folk tales collected by people such as the brothers Grimm and Andrew Lang, who had contributed to this decline, as he saw it – which is one reason why he did not like much modern literature.

Most literature for adults from the eighteenth century onwards was 'realist' in intention. **Realism** tried to represent real, everyday adult lives; it could be comic, or romantic, but not heroic. Meanwhile most fantasy literature was relegated to the nursery, while the few writers of adult fantasy such as Mary Shelley and George MacDonald were not treated seriously by

> **KEYWORD**
>
> Realism: in literature, writing that attempts to simulate peoples' experiences of the world, set in real places and times.

critics. Though he recognized the greatness of some of the children's literature of fantasy (such as *Alice in Wonderland* or *The Wind in the Willows*), Tolkien wanted nothing to do with the modern realist adult literature, which tried to copy the existing world, rather than to recreate it. However, although Tolkien's published letters make no reference to nineteenth- or twentieth-century realist novelists, we know that he read and enjoyed MacDonald; and he knew the twentieth-century fantasy writer E. R. Eddison, whose novel *The Worm Ourobouros* is among the precursors of *The Lord of the Rings*. Tolkien also read widely in science fiction, and he admired the work of Isaac Asimov among others.

TOLKIEN AT OXFORD

Most of Tolkien's professional life was spent at Oxford University. The university delivers its teaching through Colleges, which are small self-governing institutions each with its own library, dining and residential facilities; many of them are old and wealthy foundations. Academic faculty are known as 'dons' or 'fellows'. The fellowship Tolkien was awarded became a very important part of his life. It helped to produce the ideal of male companionship which is explored in *The Hobbit* and *The Lord of the Rings*. 'Fellow' is a masculine word, and in Tolkien's time all of Oxford's Colleges were single-sex institutions, so he never experienced a professional or social environment in which women were the equals of men. This may be why Tolkien's world offers us only the companionship of men. Within Tolkien's literary world, however, not all men are socially equal. Colleges had servants, and Tolkien was used to being served – as he also was when he was an army officer, by a soldier called a 'batman'. Gardener and, later, warrior Sam Gamgee, Frodo's chief companion in *The Lord of the Rings*, is an idealized College servant or army batman.

One of Tolkien's most important companions was the author C. S. Lewis, another Oxford don, a fellow Christian, and a Fellow of Magdalen College. Together, in the 1930s and beyond, they were the leading lights of the 'Inklings', an informal circle of friends which met regularly in College rooms or in Oxford pubs such as the *Eagle and Child*. This small group debated Oxford politics, life in general, and literature in particular. Members read their work aloud to their friends – Lewis read drafts of his writings such as the science fiction novel *Out of the Silent Planet*, while Tolkien read a great deal of *The Lord of the Rings*. The group discussed these drafts (though apparently Tolkien never changed his work in response to criticism). Lewis and other Inklings, sometimes including Tolkien, often holidayed together, walking through the English countryside and staying at country pubs. They all enjoyed walking, talking, drinking and smoking – these activities were crucial to their identity as English men (as well as to Tolkien's hobbits).

The Inklings at play.

TOLKIEN AND THE TWENTIETH CENTURY

Oxford University appears to be a haven of conservatism in a changing world. Many of Tolkien's critics suggest that he wrote his medieval-style fantasies because he simply rejected the modern world – and, they also suggest, his readers are therefore joining him in an act of escapism. It might indeed seem that this little group of walkers and talkers was insulated from the twentieth century. Reading their letters can give the impression that they were hiding in their Colleges' medieval cloisters while the world moved quickly onwards outside their walls (much as the elves do in Lothlórien in *The Lord of the Rings*). The Inklings would praise medieval poetry, but dismiss the latest work by T.S. Eliot, as they enjoyed a pint or two at the local pub. In a way then the Inklings *were* comparatively insulated by their privileged position, and they did indeed reject much of the modern world. However, though they disliked the modern world, they could not avoid its effects. The world events of the twentieth century had a major impact on Tolkien's work.

Tolkien lived through the two world wars which disfigured twentieth-century Europe, destroying and blighting millions of lives. He (and Lewis) served in the First World War. Tolkien became a military cadet in 1914, joined up in 1915, and as a junior officer of the 11th Lancashire Fusiliers he was present in 1916 at the Battle of the Somme. This was a catastrophic event at which some 60,000 British soldiers were killed or wounded on the first day alone, as they were ordered to march towards enemy machine gun fire. One of Tolkien's best school friends was among the dead on that terrible day, and another died a few months later. During the Second World War (1939–45), Tolkien's son Christopher fought for the British in North Africa, and during much of this time father and son corresponded, exchanging drafts of *The Lord of the Rings* in various stages of completion.

However well his College acted as an insulator from the modern world, Tolkien was also well aware of the massive social changes in twentieth-century Britain. In the 1930s, Oxford wasn't just a university town. It had become one of the centres of the British motor industry – for forty years local manufacturer Morris produced a best-selling model called the Oxford. Tolkien and his friends noted the arrival of the car both as a source of noise and as an inhibitor of their ability to walk through the countryside. Meanwhile the fields and woodlands Tolkien and his friends loved were disappearing as the demand for housing and employment led to the building of suburbs and light industrial estates. By representing the Shire as an idealized English county, and then portraying its environmental destruction and rebuilding in the final chapters of *The Lord of the Rings*, Tolkien was commenting on the world he saw around him, and his negative response to industrialization is among the beginnings of ecological thought. Through his detailed descriptions of changing landscapes, and creatures such as the hobbits and ents, Tolkien provided a new mythology for the conservation movement which emerged in the decade after *The Lord of the Rings* was published.

TOLKIEN'S LEGACY: LITERATURE AND BEYOND

The generation that came to regard *The Lord of the Rings* as great literature was the first to become aware of the environmental problems associated with industrial development and human population growth. The peaceful Shire seemed a perfect antidote to these threats. Ironically, Tolkien's work then became part of the modern popular culture which he held in suspicion. Poster designers, rock bands and night clubs began to use Tolkien iconography. Pink Floyd, whose first album *The Piper at the Gates of Dawn* was named after an episode in Kenneth Grahame's children's fantasy *The Wind in the Willows*, played at a club in West London called 'Middle Earth'. Heavy metal band Marillion was named after *The Silmarillion*. Clothing company Rohan – named after the Riders of Rohan in *The Lord of the Rings* – made outdoor wear for people who wanted to escape from the cares of urban life to the freedom of the 'wild'.

The success of *The Lord of the Rings* also led to the establishment of fantasy as a literary genre. Various writers have produced work which echoes *The Lord of the Rings*. Unfortunately most of these attempts, however long and detailed, are only pale imitations of the imaginary world of Middle-earth. More interesting have been the writers who have not tried to copy Tolkien's style but who have developed fantasy for the present day. Terry Pratchett's Discworld series, for instance, uses the building blocks of fantasy literature alongside a continuous vein of humorous contemporary social commentary. J.K. Rowling's Harry Potter stories have used elements of Tolkien's exploration of the problem of good and evil in the context of the movement from childhood to adulthood. Tolkien's representations of women are at best idealizations of a very few stereotypes, and yet both Marion Zimmer Bradley, who was among the first generation of academic critics to write in appreciation of Tolkien's work, and science fiction writer Ursula Le Guin, who has also written very positively about Tolkien's influence, have produced deliberately feminist fantasy and science fiction.

None of this literature would have been possible without the global success of *The Lord of the Rings*. But Tolkien's cultural legacy is wider than literature. There are hundreds of fantasy role-play games, from board-game or live-action versions of Dungeons and Dragons to contemporary online games in which large numbers of participants play using their own, invented, Internet identities – as warriors, witches and wizards. The Dagorhir Battle Games group, for instance, founded in the USA in 1977 and now international, stages battles between armies of people dressed as elves, orcs and so on (using padded weapons for safety).

Tolkien has always had an important presence in the world of the personal computer. Among the first adventure games for the domestic personal computers of the 1980s, such as the Sinclair ZX Spectrum and the Commodore 64, was a version of *The Hobbit*. Tolkien may well have been an Oxford conservative, out of touch with the modern world, but his work has helped to develop both the dedicated games machine such as the Playstation, the personal computer, and the Internet. Multiple-player Online Games are among the few services which people will actually pay to use online. *Warhammer* (which started as a *Lord of the Rings*-influenced board game) is among the games which have been developed for this medium.

Tolkien's legacy is also important in Hollywood, partly because his stories fit nicely with the theoretical model of narrative proposed by Joseph Campbell. Campbell was a mid-twentieth century psychologist who carried out a study of comparative mythology, noticing the similarities between various stories told in different parts of the world. His ideas are taught in film school and have become massively influential in the Hollywood movie industry. In his influential book *The Hero with a Thousand Faces*, Campbell claimed that folk tales from all over the world, and throughout history, share a very few, strong narrative outlines. For example, Our Hero, usually an orphan, is plucked from obscurity, told of his destiny by someone older and wiser than he, grows in confidence, and goes on a quest to defeat the powers of darkness. The protagonists in these narratives seek their own true identities, including the truth of their lineage, as well as the defeat of evil. Bilbo Baggins is not an orphan, but he has to go on his adventure to allow the Tookish side of his character (which he has inherited from his mother) to come through. His nephew (and orphan) Frodo goes through a similar process, though in the end his re-formed identity is less easy to live with than Bilbo's. Similar story lines can be seen in the tales of Arthur and in the Harry Potter novels and films.

Although Hollywood has made movies of *The Lord of the Rings*, Tolkien's legacy is also visible in the most popular adventure films ever made – the *Star Wars* series. The real heroes in these stories are not the big warrior princes and princesses but characters who start out as 'little people'. Luke Skywalker is in this regard like Frodo – and there are also similarities between Obiwan Kenobi and Gandalf, and Darth Vader and Sauron. Tolkien's legacy has changed the face of entertainment as a whole.

✳ ✳ ✳ *SUMMARY* ✳ ✳ ✳

- After wartime service, Tolkien lived the quiet life of an Oxford don.

- He taught language and literature.

- He invented his own languages.

- He became a successful author late in life.

- He has an important legacy in fantasy literature and popular culture.

The Major Themes 4

MAKING THE MYTHOLOGY

Tolkien's attempt to construct a 'mythology for England', using his invented languages and Old English and Northern Literature, was part of a strategy which also involved his friend C.S. Lewis and the other Inklings. They believed that 'England' was formed as a nation by the Anglo-Saxons, who invaded the British Isles in large numbers from the fifth century A.D. By the time of King Alfred, in the ninth century, there was an emerging sense of a national language and culture in most of what we now know as England. However, that culture remained fragmented – and England doesn't have a mythology of its own – largely due to the arrival of Christianity, and the invasion of the Norman French in 1066, led by William of Normandy. England became subject to a French-speaking ruling class, and lost most of its culture.

Tolkien began to write the first part of his new mythology, *The Book of Lost Tales,* during the First World War. At this point, to be English was under profound threat (military defeat could have meant another foreign occupation like the Norman French, whose effects Tolkien disliked so intensely). The absence of a collective English identity based on heroic legend was perhaps most important to Tolkien as young English manhood was being shredded, in front of his eyes, on the battlefields of the Western Front.

What, though, did Tolkien mean by a 'mythology'? It appears that according to him, the elements of mythology should include an account of the origin of earth and sky, landscape and people; of the creator who made these things; and of the entry of evil into the world. It should also include an account of the foundation of dynasties and kingdoms in a defined and recognizable geographical area, set in a time well before any recognized period of history. And, crucially, neither should it deny Christianity, nor actually be Christian, since the origin of Christianity is very specifically located in time and space, and like the Greek or Scandinavian myths, these stories should refer to a world well before Christ's arrival.

The Silmarillion obeys all these rules, and it does so because it is heavily influenced by the existing Northern European mythologies. However, Tolkien's other stories – from *The Hobbit* onwards – would have been impossible without more recent examples of nineteenth- and twentieth-century fantasy literature, including the work of George MacDonald and E.R. Eddison. But it goes beyond all these sources. Tolkien was not writing a **pastiche** of any single existing text, nor a collage of all of them. In writing *The Hobbit* and *The Lord of the Rings* he was reinventing his own mythology, so that it could cope with something new, which was much closer to the literary world he did not like: a portrayal of the ordinary man as hero.

KEYWORDS

Pastiche: a copy not of a work but of a style or technique, which tries to mimic the original as closely as possible.

Aristocracy: a ruling group which transmits its power by inheritance – such as a monarchy.

Feudalism: a relationship in which a landowner grants the use of the land to an inferior in return for favours such as military service. Such relationships were common in medieval Europe.

REWRITING THE HERO

Heroism is a vital theme in all Tolkien's work. *The Silmarillion* is about leaders: kings and queens, gods, angels and demons. They lead great armies into battle, but we hardly ever meet the ordinary soldiers. In *The Lord of the Rings* Aragorn is a great hero whose actions, which include healing as well as military success, indicate that he is the rightful heir to the kingdom of Gondor. Once this is apparent Faramir, Éomer and the other leaders swear allegiance to him. This version of heroism, then, establishes the principle of an **aristocracy** in which deserved success can be inherited, and in which leaders exist in a **feudal** system of relationships with others. This is a conservative viewpoint that angers many of Tolkien's critics. Nonetheless – and it is important to remember this when reading some of the negative criticism of Tolkien – almost all the heroes in *The Silmarillion* (perhaps Beren and Lúthien, and Eärendil are exceptions) are deeply flawed. More importantly, in *The Hobbit* and *The Lord of the Rings* Tolkien's mythology is seen through the eyes not of Gandalf or Aragorn but of the little man who muddles through.

In most of the stories published in Tolkien's lifetime the ordinary man is 'hero'. Bilbo, Farmer Giles, Niggle and Frodo, are all comfortable when we first meet them, living stress-free lives, unwilling to take risks, uncertain and shy. They are all willing to take direction from people they perceive to be wiser than themselves. Even Smith of Wootton Major doesn't push his luck in the world of Faërie. Most of these characters come through in the end – but they don't often act heroically. Unlike the genuinely heroic Túrin Turambar in *The Silmarillion* (who kills the dragon Glaurung, Bilbo and Farmer Giles don't fight their respective dragons, but get what they want with a combination of smart talk and good luck. Bilbo is knocked out early in the battle of the Five Armies. Frodo fights on Weathertop, and strikes the first blow against the troll in Moria, but he later throws away his weapons, and refuses to fight on his return to the Shire even though he concedes that fighting is necessary; others have to do it. He is wounded, stung, captured, and in the end he can't even destroy the Ring by himself. This is a very qualified heroism.

A MULTICULTURAL MYTHOLOGY

Tolkien's mythology departs from the Northern European models in one other important respect. The sources Tolkien drew on tended to start with the creation of the world and progressed to rivalries among families, dynasties and nations. In the Northern European model elves, dwarves, trolls and goblins are tricksters or tempters outside the principal world of the story, which is the human drama. Tolkien's mythology is bound up with the very different, and often very difficult, allegiances and mixing of different species or 'races': this makes his

Middle-earth a very different place from the Midgard of the Icelandic *Sagas*, for example, which saw the triumphs and disasters of families such as the Nibelungs. Although it might be an inappropriate **anachronism** to use the contemporary term 'multicultural' about Tolkien's created world, we can certainly call him anti-racist. In his valedictory address in 1959 (on retiring from Oxford University) Tolkien announced 'I have the hatred of **apartheid** in my bones'. He clearly desired that very different groups of beings, with very different languages and cultures, could and should get along. In Tolkien's world, elves and dwarves often quarrel grievously, and at times make war on each other, but they join forces against evil. The nine companions who set out to help Frodo to destroy the Ring are chosen by

KEYWORDS

Anachronism: something which seems to be in the wrong time – a horse and cart on a motorway, for example.

KEY FACT

Apartheid: this refers to the political system in South Africa which ended in 1990, in which white and black people were kept entirely separate for all social, legal and political purposes, in an attempt to preserve the whites' rule over the blacks.

Elrond as representatives of the 'free peoples'. 'Elves, Dwarves, and Men. Forth the Three Hunters', cries Aragorn at the start of Book 3 of *The Lord of The Rings* (Book III, Chapter 1), while a few days later the hobbits Merry and Pippin forge a new alliance with the ents, which leads to the downfall of Saruman.

THE LONG DEFEAT

At the end of *The Lord of the Rings* the continuance on earth of most of these species is open to doubt. This sense of loss pervades both *The Silmarillion* and *The Lord of the Rings*, as it does in most Anglo-Saxon poetry. Galadriel refers to 'the long defeat' the elves have fought against (*The Lord of the Rings*, Book II, Chapter 7). The final destruction of Sauron is only a temporary victory, like the victories before it. Evil will rise again. Wise and powerful characters such as Fëanor and Saruman are incapable of sustaining their creativity and wisdom; each is corrupted by dreams of power. The Shire is renewed at the end of *The*

Lord of the Rings – but the unstained beauty of Lothlórien fades, because the Ring has been destroyed. The elves are a tragic people, wise, beautiful and immortal, but corrupted by their own creative efforts (the Silmarils and the Three Rings), which cause the wars that have led to their own downfall. Despite their beauty and despite lives of learning which last for many thousands of years, they do not realize their potential.

Corruption and greed, leading to social decay, are almost universal themes in Tolkien's world. The disputes over treasure in *The Hobbit* indicate that elves, dwarves and men, as well as wolves and goblins, can share the same greedy desires which led the dragon Smaug to drive the dwarves from the Lonely Mountain in the first place. Though there are characters who seem purely good – notably Gandalf after his resurrection – few are in fact totally pure. The Númenorians of the Second Age, obsessed by mortality, decline from civilized greatness. They cease to acknowledge the Valar's authority, and their civilization is destroyed. The death of Arwen and her bitter final parting from her father represent the pain of choices made through love. Over all Tolkien's writing hovers a sense that all that is good on earth will come to an end:

> Where now the horse and the rider? Where is the horn that was
> blowing?
> Where is the helm and the hauberk, and the bright hair flowing?
> Where is the hand on the harpstring, and the red fire glowing?
>   (*The Lord of the Rings*, Book III, Chapter 6)

This, recited by Aragorn, is a poem of the Rohirrim. It is based on the Anglo-Saxon poems *The Seafarer* and *The Wanderer*, which mourn the corrosive passing of time.

MYTHOLOGY AND CHRISTIANITY

Although the theme of loss in Tolkien's work draws on his awareness of the pagan English culture, his work is also deeply influenced by his Christian beliefs. Most of the stories are not directly religious in the

Where now the rider, and the horn that was blowing?

same way as C. S. Lewis's Narnia books – it is easy to read them without noticing their religious content – but Christian stories are a background source for Tolkien's work.

The Silmarillion repeats the story of the **Fall**, when the enormous potential of Man is blighted by the coming of evil into the world. Good opposes evil throughout the book, and the evil is generated by a spirit who has deviated from the will of God: this is a retelling of Satan's rebellion in heaven. The original elves in Middle-earth are like Adam and Eve in Eden. The corruption of Fëanor by Melkor is a

KEYWORD

Fall: the Biblical story of the entry of evil into the world. Satan persuades Eve to taste the forbidden fruit. She then persuades Adam to taste it, and as a result the couple are banished from Paradise.

retelling of the Fall of Man, and the corruption of good by evil is a recurring constant thereafter. Melkor corrupts Fëanor, Sauron's deceitful claims bring about the downfall of Númenor, and Sauron destroys the integrity of Saruman. In a smaller way Sauron's ring corrupts many of those who deal with it, including Gollum, Boromir and to an extent even Frodo. The corrupted pay the price, however good, wise, powerful and creative they were before they were corrupted – Fëanor, Saruman, and Boromir all die, and none achieve their goal.

Since there is absolute evil in the world, and since it can corrupt anyone, the good must oppose it. Tolkien's world can therefore have no place for pacifism: he believed in the concept of the 'just war' (and he believed that those of 1914–18 and 1939–45 were justified opposition to evil regimes, though he was horrified by the saturation bombing of German cities and the atomic bombing of Japanese cities). The good must be ready to sacrifice themselves in a just war. The Dead, who refused to fight Sauron at the beginning of the Third Age, are only released from their ghosthood when they have redeemed their pledge and fought against his allies at the end of the Age, under Aragorn's command. Beren and Lúthien, Gandalf, and Frodo all give their lives for the greater good. But though they are all resurrected and allowed to pass on to heavenly rewards, they first encounter death.

LOVE AND CHARITY
Love is an ever-present quality in Tolkien's work, though it is usually 'love' as in Christ's additions to the ten commandments – he enjoined his followers to 'love your neighbour as yourself'. Christ's early follower St Paul claimed that in doing so 'charity' is the greatest form of love, and more important than sexual or family love. This can be seen in Tolkien's work through love for one person, as well as the collective sacrifice for everyone made by Gandalf. Sam is prepared to sacrifice the whole mission – and rescues Frodo from torture that would have revealed the plan to destroy the Ring – thanks to his love for Frodo.

Love in *The Lord of the Rings* is principally asexual love among men. There is also romantic love between men and women – between Aragorn and Arwen, or Sam and Rosie Cotton. However, apart from the fierce flicker of Éowyn's frustrated desire for Aragorn, there is hardly even a hint of sexual desire, even as corruption; Tolkien's mythology seems to have no direct equivalent to Eve. Sex as a disruptive force does, occasionally, occur in his work, as in the tragic story of Túrin Turambar and Niniel (Chapter 21 of *The Silmarillion*). They kill themselves when they discover that they are brother and sister and have unknowingly had an incestuous marriage. However, it is worth noting that this story is not original to Tolkien but based on the story of Kullervo in the *Kalevala*. Otherwise, in figures such as Lúthien and Arwen we have women who sacrifice their immortal lives for the love of mortal men. Other female characters are either sexless goddesses such as Galadriel or Goldberry, or sexless middle-aged women, such as Mrs Maggot or Ioreth. This lack of attention to sex, which is such a fundamental, important and disruptive aspect of humanity, is presumably due to Tolkien's deep Catholic beliefs in the sanctity of marriage and in sexual fidelity – chastity – which would not allow him to explore the alternatives. C. S. Lewis, another conservative, even puritanical writer, has far more of a sense of the importance of sexual desire – as you can find in the closing chapter of his science fiction novel *That Hideous Strength*, which is roughly contemporary with *The Lord of the Rings*.

Love instead appears in *The Lord of the Rings* as pity – one of the forms of charitable love. Bilbo, Gandalf, Frodo and Sam, and Faramir, all refrain from killing Gollum; Gollum himself has a similar moment of love for Frodo, touching him gently when he is asleep when he could have killed him and stolen the Ring instead. Pity distinguishes them all from Sauron, and therefore diminishes the power of the One Ring to rule them all and bind them in Sauron's service. The characters are indeed bound together, and all have to combine to defeat Sauron, because of the love for all which generates pity. This is why Frodo cannot order Saruman's destruction. The power for these judgements is in the end deferred to the One God; who alone can untangle the weave that binds all, in Middle-earth, together.

THE GREEN MAN

Tolkien's mythology is implicitly and deeply Christian, then. But Tolkien's work can also be seen as **pagan**; indeed, in his insistence on the importance of the natural world, Tolkien makes his most radical departure from the sources for his 'mythology'. His work constantly stresses the importance of a functioning **ecology**. He sees trees as the equals of people, and many of his animals and birds can speak. Nature gods Tom Bombadil and Lady Goldberry, the barrow-wights, the ents, and Old Man Willow, are all powerful and original creations which are parts of the landscape rather than parts of societies. But for the interpreters of Tolkien's work they are more difficult to deal with than the elves, dwarves and dragons which he drew or redrew from existing sources. The adaptations of *The Lord of the Rings* – including the BBC radio adaptation as well as both the film versions – leave Tom Bombadil and Goldberry out altogether. The Green side of Tolkien's work detracts from the focus on action.

KEYWORDS

Pagan: the worship of nature and the seasons.

Ecology: the balance of the natural world, including the lives and deaths of all living things.

Romanticism: an early nineteenth-century movement, which celebrated the beauty of the natural world and peoples' potential for freedom.

In his use of nature Tolkien was close to the composer Richard Wagner – probably rather closer than he wanted to be. Tolkien loathed the ways in which Wagner had adapted Icelandic and Germanic sources for his four-evening opera *The Ring of the Nibelung.* Tolkien's attitude towards the natural world, like Wagner's, is derived from nineteenth-century **Romanticism,** not from the heroic poetry and romances that both men used as their source material. In these sources, the natural environment is a backdrop, mentioned in passing (if at all) rather than described in detail; in Tolkien's and Wagner's work it is celebrated. Tolkien was influenced by William Morris, an English craftsman, architect and writer who acknowledged Wagner's influence, and who also took more pains to describe the natural environment than the original authors of the Sagas when he wrote his own versions of them.

If the celebration of the trees, and of animals such as the eagles, the horse Shadowfax and Bill the pony can be seen as both pagan and romantic, they are also celebrations of God's work. The 'Ainulindalë', the first section of *The Silmarillion*, shows how the earth is created by a woven melody, and how the angelic Valar then provide the world's natural environment. The world and its inhabitants (including Morgoth and the orcs) are *creatures* – most of them are literally created by the music of the One. Thus Tolkien's apparently pagan celebration of nature is in fact a part of his Christianity.

There is another important aspect of Tolkien's ecological thought – one which encouraged his status as a cult figure in the later 1960s. At this point in time political awareness about damage to the environment caused by industrial pollution and population growth was intensifying: people were harming the earth. The Shire is quite clearly intended to be a representation of a pre-industrial rural England in which people and environment are in balance. It is one of a number of landscapes, including those of the idealized Lothlórien, and the potentially ideal Ithilien, which Tolkien represents as good because they do or could blend well-tended natural growth with human habitation. The wildernesses, however, are not always so positive – mountains are cruel and inhospitable; the Old Forest, though tameable by Tom Bombadil, is unsafe for its hobbit visitors, and Fangorn forest is also dangerous for anyone who ventures into it without the approval of Treebeard. Tolkien also represents landscapes ruined by the actions of men, elves, dwarves and orcs. These places are often terrible – such as the Barrow Downs, the Dead Marshes, and especially the desolation before the gates of Mordor: 'here nothing lived, not even the leprous growths that feed on rottenness' (*The Lord of the Rings*, Book IV, Chapter 2).

Pity stays his hand.

Tolkien had actually experienced landscapes like this during the First World War. The poignancy of this human capacity to destroy the best of both human and natural environments is demonstrated at the end of *The Lord of the Rings* when the hobbits return to the Shire, and find a mill which is belching forth industrial pollution, in a landscape of destroyed trees and ruined houses which echoes Tolkien's wartime experiences. The obvious delight of the old miller's son, Ted Sandyman, who revels in the new power of the machines, adds to the sadness. Another example is the industrialization of Isengard and the making of the new breed of orc-men (represented brilliantly in the Peter Jackson film *The Fellowship of the Ring*). The ents' destruction of Isengard, and its rebuilding as a green, tree-filled space, are among the most deeply-felt evocations of natural beauty in the book; Treebeard and Elrond agree that one day there will be a greener future which will echo the beauties of the past: 'There in the willow-meads of Tasarinan we will walk in the Spring' (*The Lord of the Rings*, Book VI, Chapter 6).

In a book which deliberately connects ecology and landscape with the workings of the plot, Sam's re-greening of the Shire is also an act of revenge for the barbarism which has happened to the Shire. It is hard to think of any previous fictional tale in which maps and landscapes are so important. It is worth remembering that for Tolkien and friends walking, talking and drinking were part of their shared masculinity. C. S. Lewis's ideal holiday was a long walk, with the evening spent at a friendly inn at the end of the day. The Inklings experienced the gradual loss of this particular version of England. Even as Tolkien assembled the mythology, much of the landscape they loved was being suburbanized. It did not quite become Mordor, but in their eyes Oxford began to look like the industrialized Isengard – and they did not like it.

So Tolkien was an important early ecological thinker. He gave up driving when he saw the damage that roads were doing to his beloved countryside – and he never owned a washing machine or a television set. But there is a paradox in his behaviour. Unlike T.H. White, say, (a contemporary fantasy writer who had similar views on the impact of the motor car and the suburb), Tolkien did not live in the countryside. Instead he was a suburban dweller, living most of his adult life in Oxford suburbs, and retiring briefly to a bungalow in Poole, a suburb of Bournemouth. He remembered the country cottage of his childhood (which had become part of a Birmingham suburb) as a Paradise lost. The mythology of Middle-earth, including its landscapes, he knew very well was part of the past, whatever its theological or ecological status as 'truth'.

✷ ✷ ✷ SUMMARY ✷ ✷ ✷

Tolkien's work helps us to think about:

- the nature of heroism.

- religion in a world before Christianity.

- ecology – the whole world, not just humans.

The Major Works

Tolkien wrote poetry and short stories all his life, and many of his works have been published posthumously. But while some of these (such as *Roverandom*, *Mr Bliss* or the *Father Christmas Letters*) are charming, they have little to do with his chief storytelling effort. For the purposes of this chapter his stories can be grouped into three: the two hobbit stories (which connect the mythology with Tolkien's version of the modern world), the mythological work itself, and the partly autobiographical short stories which explore the author's identity as a writer of fantasy.

THE HOBBIT

The Hobbit is a children's story which uses the story of Middle-earth as deep background; it can be read without any knowledge or understanding of the history of Middle-earth. But as if by accident it also begins the story of *The Lord of the Rings*. We meet a wide range of humanoid species – hobbits, a wizard, dwarves, trolls, goblins and elves – and other sentient creatures such as a thrush who can understand human speech, and a crow, and eagles, who can speak it; groups of hostile wolves and spiders; and of course a proud and very dangerous dragon. But first of all we meet hobbits – who, unlike the other species in the book, are not part of Scandinavian legend but drawn from Tolkien's mind; they were invented for this story.

Bilbo Baggins is a very comfortable and relaxed hobbit. He lives in a spacious and well-decorated hole in Hobbiton, the chief town of the Shire – a region of the world rather like rural Warwickshire, where Tolkien lived as a boy. Hobbits are very like people, and through them Tolkien connects his mythological world with at least one idealized version of the modern world. Bilbo is obviously well off, though we never learn whether he is a farmer or trader, or whether his money is inherited; either way he need never do anything exciting, and he claims that like most Shire folk he doesn't want to. But the wizard Gandalf sees in him the capacity for action, and in the opening chapter, 'An Unexpected Party', Bilbo is persuaded to join a company of dwarves led by Thorin Oakenshield on an adventure. The company leaves the Shire, with its comfort zone of perpetual mealtimes, and sets off into the wild to reclaim the dwarves' treasure, which is guarded by a dragon at the Lonely Mountain. They meet and defeat three trolls, before resting at Rivendell, the last homely house before the Misty Mountains, where they encounter friendly (and rather silly) elves led by the wise Elrond, who provides help. Once in the mountains they encounter a group of goblins, who drag them into the mountains' underground passages, and while they are escaping from them Bilbo becomes detached from the rest of the group and wanders along in the dark. He finds a ring, and pockets it before he meets Gollum, a small but dangerous hobbit-like creature who has lost the ring. After a game of riddles, Bilbo realizes that the ring has magical properties (it renders its wearer invisible) and he escapes from Gollum. Once again the company rests and recuperates, this time as the guests of the shapeshifting Beorn (a man who can turn himself into a bear).

Possessing the magic ring helps Bilbo to rescue the dwarves from man-eating spiders, and also from the unfriendly wood-elves they encounter in the forest of Mirkwood. The company spend some time recovering at Laketown (where they encounter men – ordinary humans – for the first time on the quest) before their final journey to the Lonely Mountain. The ring gives Bilbo the courage to face the mighty Smaug, the dragon who guards the treasure he has stolen from the dwarves; during their conversation Bilbo learns that there is a weak link in Smaug's armour. Thinking he knows where Bilbo has come from, Smaug destroys Laketown; but a crow informs Bard, the town's best bowman, where to shoot, and the dragon is killed. The Lakemen and elves then demand a share of the treasure. The dwarves refuse to give it up; and even when Bilbo secretly negotiates, giving the Lakemen and elves a jewel desired by Thorin to use as a bargaining counter, the dwarves won't give way.

Bilbo (nearly) meets his match.

A siege begins. However, the goblins and wolves of the Misty Mountains attack, and the dwarves, elves and men, later joined by the eagles, combine to defeat them in the Battle of the Five Armies. Thorin is killed, and the treasure is shared; the dwarves re-establish themselves in the mineworkings of the Lonely Mountain, and Bard leads the rebuilding of Laketown. Bilbo returns to the Shire a wealthier, wiser and happier man. And he keeps the ring.

The language used in *The Hobbit* is, for Tolkien, simple. The story rests lightly on the history of Middle-earth; anyone can read and enjoy it without the framework of history provided in the longer works. It is different from Tolkien's other long stories in that it is organized around a number of key scenes which are dominated by repetitive, almost ritualistic games. The company assembles gradually, by ones and twos, several times: at the first appearance of the dwarves at Bilbo's house, at the encounter with the trolls, and at Beorn's hall. In the centre of the text is Bilbo's riddle game with Gollum, and the final third of the book begins with Bilbo's equally tricky verbal and riddle-dominated confrontation with Smaug. This way of structuring a narrative plays no part in the other long stories.

Even though the narrative structure in *The Hobbit* is unique, it is connected to Tolkien's longer tales in several respects. It is full of poetry, reminding us that Tolkien is not describing a literate culture, dominated by the printed word, or by the computer's memory chip, but an oral culture, in which rhymes are an important aid to memory. And *The Hobbit* provides three important links to *The Lord of the Rings*. Firstly, *The Hobbit* provides the Ring, which Tolkien came to realize was a Ring of Power which could be woven into an altogether bigger and darker tale. Secondly it introduces Gandalf. Though at first he seems to be a less powerful (and more comical) figure than he is in *The Lord of the Rings*, by the end of *The Hobbit* we learn that the wizard has been involved in important affairs. He has interviewed a dying dwarf chieftain, which leads him to call together forces that expel the Necromancer from Dol Goldur. Through these few lines towards the end of *The Hobbit* a small window opens onto the wider history of Middle-earth, and on re-reading *The Hobbit* after *The Lord of the Rings*, the reader can appreciate these links more fully. Thirdly, *The Hobbit* introduces 'the hobbit'. Hobbits provide an important character type, which is Tolkien's most important variation (of 'ordinary folk') on the epic mythologies of the *Silmarillion*. Bilbo is not a hero – in fact in many ways he is an 'anti-hero'. He is small, chubby, unromantic, cowardly much of the time (and only really brave when he has the Ring on). He cannot fight, or win the hand of a fair maid like a hero; and he does not fully share either the dwarves' obsession for wealth, or Gandalf's wisdom, or the elves' sense of fun or beauty. He is something of an outsider, even at the end, when he is unknowingly the proud owner of a Ring of Power.

THE LORD OF THE RINGS
The Lord of the Rings began as a sequel to *The Hobbit*, and its opening is deceptively similar, including the first chapter's title, 'A Long-

expected Party'. Once again we meet Bilbo, in his comfortable hole at the heart of the Shire, as he plans his 111th birthday party alongside his orphaned nephew Frodo. Gandalf arrives, to provide a few fireworks, and the wizard warns Bilbo to give up the Ring, which has become an object of obsessive desire for him. After a difficult psychological struggle, Bilbo does so, and leaves the Shire. Twenty years later Gandalf returns, and explains to Frodo why Bilbo – like Gollum – had become obsessed with the Ring. It was forged in volcanic fire by Sauron, the ancient evil ruler who we met in *The Hobbit* as the Necromancer. By torturing Gollum in his fortress in the land of Mordor, Sauron learns that his device has been found. Gandalf warns Frodo to take the Ring from the Shire.

Frodo, his servant Sam, and friends Merry and Pippin duly leave the Shire. In the Old Forest they meet malevolent trees, and outside the Forest they are captured by evil barrow-wights; they are rescued from each peril by Tom Bombadil – a fearless nature god. But Bombadil will not accompany them, and as they journey on they are tracked by fearsome riders wearing black – Nazgûl, the emissaries of Sauron. Luckily they fall under the protection of Strider, a friend of Gandalf. Nonetheless the Black Riders attack, wounding Frodo, and the company reaches Rivendell only just in time for Elrond's medical skills to save him. Gandalf is already here – as is Bilbo, who reveals to Frodo that 'Strider' is in fact Aragorn, the heir of Isildur, who had cut the Ring from Sauron's hand thousands of years ago. Therefore Aragorn is also the heir to the kingdom of Gondor. A council of wizard, men, dwarves and elves is informed that war is being prepared by Mordor, and that the wizard Saruman desires the Ring for himself. The council concludes that the only course of action is to take the Ring to the volcano where it was forged and destroy it – which they assume will also destroy Sauron. Frodo agrees to take the Ring.

Gandalf, the four hobbits, the men Aragorn and Boromir, the dwarf Gimli, and the elf Legolas journey south. Bad weather defeats their attempt to cross the mountains, so instead they journey through the abandoned dwarf-kingdom of Moria. Goblins (now relabelled orcs) attack them, and they escape only to confront the reason the dwarves had left Moria: a balrog – a demonic wizard from a far earlier age. Gandalf and the balrog appear to fall to their deaths while fighting on a bridge.

The remaining eight enter the elvish forest-land of Lothlórien. Here time seems to stand still. Celeborn and Galadriel, Lothlórien's ancient but young-looking rulers, provide assistance. But Galadriel has also tested their constancy, and the test proves too much for Boromir, who begins to desire the Ring, thinking that he can wield it in the defence of his city Minas Tirith, the capital of Gondor. He tries to take the Ring from Frodo, who escapes, leaves the company with Sam, and journeys towards Mordor. This is the end of the first volume of the trilogy, *The Fellowship of the Ring*.

A band of orcs attacks the party, and Boromir dies defending the two remaining hobbits, who are captured. The orcs are destroyed by the Rohirrim or Riders of Rohan, golden-haired horsemen who speak a language very like Anglo-Saxon. Their captain, Éomer, befriends Aragorn, Legolas and Gimli. Merry and Pippin enter Fangorn forest, where they meet Treebeard, an 'ent' – a tree-like being who acts as a guardian of trees. The ents decide to help in the defeat of Saruman, who has attacked Rohan. Aragorn, Legolas and Gimli discover some of this when they meet Gandalf once more. He tells them that he had eventually defeated the balrog, but his own body had failed; however he had been 'sent back' by the powers senior to him, who wished him to lead the fight against Sauron. The four meet Théoden, the King of Rohan, and help him to defeat Saruman.

Meanwhile Frodo and Sam meet up with Gollum, who acts as a useful but untrustworthy guide. They travel through a variety of hostile landscapes before they reach Ithilien, a still-pleasant part of Gondor at the edge of Mordor. Here they meet Boromir's brother Faramir, a captain of Gondor's army. He too provides help, and the three travel on up a dangerous path towards the site of Gollum's treachery. He has planned to deliver the hobbits to Shelob, a huge spider who he thinks will eat them and then throw away whatever trinkets they were carrying, and thus he will get the Ring back. No such luck – Frodo is paralysed by Shelob's sting, but Sam forces her to retreat. Then Sam leaves Frodo, takes the Ring and enters Mordor, intending to do the deed of destruction himself. Thus ends the second volume of the trilogy, *The Two Towers*.

The victors.

In a battle outside Minas Tirith, the Rohirrim and Aragorn's forces win the day after Merry and King Théoden's sister's daughter, Éowyn, kill the Lord of the Nazgûl. The Western forces then march on Mordor, hoping to draw Sauron's attention away from what is happening inside his borders. Sam rescues Frodo from quarrelling orcs, and the hobbits slowly and painfully make their way to the mountain and enter the chamber which Sauron had constructed as his forge. Here Frodo realizes that he has become too obsessed by the Ring to destroy it. He puts it on. But Gollum, still following, bites the Ring (plus finger) from Frodo's hand, triumphantly dances on the edge of the fire, and falls into it. The mission is accomplished.

There are exultant feasts, coronations, weddings and reunions, and the company parts for the last time. But meanwhile the Shire has fallen under the sway of Saruman, who has to be defeated once more; after a brief battle, Saruman is killed by one of his own followers. Sam, Merry and Pippin earn fame and fortune as the Shire returns to prosperity, but Frodo is too wounded by his experiences to enjoy the rebuilding of the Shire. Two years later he meets with Bilbo, Gandalf and a company of elves, and all leave the shores of Middle-earth to seek peace elsewhere. This is the end of the third volume, *The Return of the King*.

The first thing the contemporary reader notices about *The Lord of the Rings* is the language. The opening of *The Lord of the Rings* is a *Hobbit*-like children's story, in which slightly grumpy hobbits prepare for a party and then everyone enjoys it. But even here Tolkien is quietly preparing us for the rest of the work's seriousness. Many of the sentences use a technique drawn from the Anglo-Saxon poetry he loved, **alliteration**. For example, after Bilbo has disappeared, 'one hundred and forty-four flabbergasted hobbits sat back speechless' (Book I, Chapter 1). This use of an old style – that of alliteration – tells us that the heroic and tragic past is already present at this jolly party

KEYWORDS

Alliteration: a sequence of words with the same letter or sound.

Archaic: characteristic of a much earlier period – in Tolkien's case this means using old-fashioned words and grammar.

Psalm: a song of praise to God. The Psalms form the twentieth Book of the Old Testament of the Holy Bible.

(in the form of the Ring Bilbo has just put on). In the next chapter, 'The Shadow of the Past', the language becomes more formal and heroic as Gandalf explains the world's peril. From this point on the style becomes increasingly **archaic**, until by the third volume the language echoes the Standard Authorized version of the Bible. When we are invited to look at something, the narrator emphasizes its importance with 'lo!' or 'behold!'; and when the eagle arrives to tell the people of Minas Tirith that Sauron has been defeated he sings a verse that is very like a **psalm**:

Sing and rejoice, ye people of the Tower of Guard,
For your watch hath not been in vain,
And the Black Gate is broken,
And your King has passed through, and he is victorious
                                        (Book VI, Chapter 5)

The language used therefore echoes the development of the plot. After the Ring has been identified, the Shire is no longer a comfort zone suitable for birthday parties, and the arrival of the Black Riders confirms its loss of innocence and safety. There is then a desperate search for survival, led by Aragorn, until the council at Rivendell decides that there is no comfort zone left anywhere. If the Ring is not destroyed the world will fall to Sauron altogether. The question then remains – given that the world's wickedness has now made contact with the Shire, how will the act of destruction be accomplished, and who will accomplish it? Here Tolkien continues his exploration of the nature of heroism, juxtaposing ordinary hobbits against legendary heroes. In many ways the hobbits stand for people like us. Merry and Pippin are tricksters, not taking the quest seriously: 'fool of a Took! ... Throw yourself in next time!', cries Gandalf as Pippin idly throws a stone into the well in Moria (Book IV, Chapter 4). They connect themselves more closely with the quest by meeting Treebeard, and by fighting; but they return to the Shire still light-hearted and ordinary.

Sam is a very important character. Like Bilbo in *The Hobbit*, he connects the mythological world with the real one. In Ithilien, Sam is made to speak as a modern man, talking casually about 'fish and chips' (in Book IV, Chapter 4) while the rest of the characters are still using archaic language. Sam therefore connects the reader to the story in a way that Tolkien never tries to do in *The Silmarillion*. Sam also acts as a kind of narrator, prompting other characters to explain parts of the history of Middle-earth. And as the hobbits approach Mordor he actually imagines the story he is a part of. Finally it is Sam who finishes the Red Book of Westmarch when Frodo departs: he writes the story we are reading.

The story also has old-style heroes. Although he is highly self-critical, Aragorn hardly puts a foot wrong from the moment we first meet him in the inn at Bree until he inherits his kingdom. Legolas, Gimli, Faramir and Éomer also do little wrong; but as a hero who has failed, Boromir has to die. Gandalf meanwhile starts the story as a powerful character but not a prime mover. By his own admission there is much that he does not understand. But after he has been transformed into Gandalf the White, he acts as if in complete command of every situation. He is a hero of the story; but he does not destroy the Ring. For that we need Gollum, a figure who bridges the worlds of anti-hero and pure evil; and who survives to bite the Ring from Frodo's hand because of the unheroic, charitable pity of several of those who have met him along the way.

The story is not directly part of the mythology which Tolkien worked on for most of his life, but it is far closer to that world than *The Hobbit*. Again we see the importance of oral culture. Characters tell stories of themselves – which allow them and their audience to reflect on their own identities whether as hobbits, dwarves, elves, ents or men. The stories and verse introduce aspects of Middle-earth's history, reinforcing the mythology's central ideas of heroism and sacrifice in order to triumph over evil, and the inevitable decay of past civilizations. These stories support the characters' identities, and help to drive them on to their own heroic and sacrificial deeds.

The end of the book offers a bridge to the rest of the invented mythology which, far more than *The Lord of the Rings*, was Tolkien's life's work. *The Lord of the Rings* closes with a number of appendices (the actual number depends on the edition) which provide supplementary information on the events of the story, the languages spoken by the various principal creatures, and chronologies of Middle-earth's three Ages. The reader who has looked through these will be ready to tackle *The Silmarillion*.

THE SILMARILLION

Tolkien died before the publication of *The Silmarillion*. He had tried to have a version of it published at the same time as *The Lord of the Rings*, but when two publishers turned it down he carried on rewriting it until his death. The volume we know as *The Silmarillion* – which many Tolkien fans claim to be the most important and profound of all his writings – was published in an edition prepared for publication by his son, Christopher, who had helped his father in the last years of his life while *The Silmarillion* was being revised yet again. The book comes complete with a very comprehensive index and a selective guide to the Elvish languages.

The Silmarillion is very different from the richly woven narrative of *The Lord of the Rings*. It is equally rich, but it is not a straightforward story moving from beginning to end. Again, the work is consciously archaic, but the archaism is deliberately much less consistent than in *The Lord of the Rings*. The author wishes us to think that the book is a mixture of different records written down at different times by different people. He has mixed what seems to be pure myth and legend – for instance, stories about the first appearance of sun and moon or stories which try to explain why there are particular stars in the sky – with what seems to be orthodox history, describing people who have played their parts in rival factions, in court politics, or in warfare. There are several different versions of the same stories (and there are more of the same in *Unfinished Tales* and the other work edited by Christopher Tolkien).

As we have it, however, *The Silmarillion* begins very logically, at the very beginning – with a brief story, 'Ainulindalë'. This is Tolkien's story of the creation of the world; and within a page of the creation, we also see the entry of evil into the world. In the beginning was music. The One being, Ilúvatar (or God) calls into existence a number of lesser beings, the Ainur, who learn their identities – their place in the order of existence – by singing their own melodies, which are given to them by the One, and then by listening to the others as they sing in turn.

Then the One invites them all to sing together, and all is good until Melkor, one of the Ainur, starts to sing a tune of his own devising. The result is chaos rather than harmony; this first discord leads eventually to Melkor's disengagement and independence from the One and the rest of the Ainur. And yet this song – including Melkor's contribution – has created a new world, Arda: the Earth. Another short section called 'Valaquenta' follows with a descriptive account of the Earth's guardian spirits, the Valar, and their less powerful assistants, the Maiar, and their opponents led by Melkor.

The 'Quenta Silmarillion' itself begins with the peopling of this new world, and with the continuous conflicts between good and evil which have characterized its history. The Valar light the world with two lamps, and plant the seeds of vegetable and animal life. The lamps are destroyed by Melkor, and much of the world's beauty is destroyed. The Valar retreat to their own land, Valinor; while Valinor is lit by two trees, Middle-earth remains in twilight as the first of the elves are given life by Ilúvatar. Melkor immediately captures some of them and tortures and twists their bodies and minds, creating the orcs in mockery of the elves' beauty. To protect the elves the Valar drive Melkor from the boundaries of Middle-earth and imprison him. While some of the elves then go to Valinor, others remain in Middle-earth, where they meet the dwarves who have also awoken. In effect the elves are divided into tribes or nations, and much of the subsequent narrative concerns rivalries and blood-feuds among them.

At this point – Chapter 6 – we meet Fëanor, the first genuine character in the story who is allowed character traits beyond good, evil and gender. Fëanor is born in one of these elvish tribes, the Noldor, and Tolkien makes some effort here to go beyond the shadowy and legendary descriptions he has so far provided of the One God, his lieutenants the angelic Valar and Maiar, their satanic opponents led by Melkor, and the first elves. Fëanor is both good and bad, and from this point on all the elves, dwarves and men we meet are also flawed characters. Fëanor is immensely knowledgeable and skilful, but also proud and stubborn. He makes the Silmarils – jewels that contain the light of the trees of Valinor. Melkor, meanwhile, has been released from imprisonment, tries to befriend the Noldor, then spreads rumours among them. They split into factions and forge weapons for the first time. Helped by the spider Ungoliant, Melkor destroys the two trees and steals the Silmarils, and Fëanor and his brothers vow to regain them, whoever stands in their way. They rename Melkor Morgoth, 'the enemy'. Most of the Noldor follow Fëanor back to Middle-earth. They take ships from another tribe of elves, the Teleri, by force, before making war on Morgoth. Fëanor is killed by balrogs, and the dying elf renews his curse, urging his kindred to pursue their cause whatever the cost.

The Valar create the sun and moon from the last leaves of the two dying trees, and the first men awake under the light of the sun. Despite their differences – men are mortal and elves are immortal unless killed in battle – many men become allies of the elves against Morgoth. Among them is Beren, who falls in love with an elf, Lúthien. Here the story broadens out, and for a while the narrative style is closer to that of *The Lord of the Rings*. Friendships and worthy deeds are explored as well as reported; there is more dialogue and poetry. While Lúthien enchants Morgoth, Beren takes a Silmaril from Morgoth's crown; but soon Beren is killed. Lúthien pleads before the Valar: 'For Luthien wove two themes

The lovers.

of words, of the sorrow of the Eldar and the grief of Men, of the two kindreds that were made by Ilúvatar to dwell in Arda, the Kingdom of Earth amid the innumerable stars.' (Chapter 19). Beren and Lúthien are permitted a second, mortal life in Middle-earth.

War is made on Morgoth once again, but strife among men, dwarves and elves for the possession of Beren's Silmaril allows Morgoth to destroy Doriath and Gondolin, the last kingdoms of the Elves. Bearing the Silmaril, Eärendil and Elwing cross the seas and plead the cause of the elves and men before the Valar. Eärendil takes the Silmaril aloft as a star, while the Valar return to Middle-earth and this time banish Morgoth from Arda altogether. The two remaining Silmarils are buried in the earth and the depths of the sea. Thus ends the 'Quenta Silmarillion', Tolkien's story of the First Age of Middle-earth.

The Silmarillion continues with brief accounts of the subsequent two Ages. These are much more orthodox – the closer they are to the present, the more the stories read like history and less like mythology. 'Akallabeth' recounts the history of the Second Age, when the men who had fought against Morgoth alongside the elves are rewarded with an island within sight of Valinor – though they are forbidden from sailing towards it. This is the kingdom of Númenor, and for a long while it flourishes as a centre of trade, scholarship and learning, and friendship between men and elves. But the Númenorians begin to desire the immortality they thought that the Valar could give them, and their lives grow shorter. They defeat Morgoth's former lieutenant Sauron, who had become a power in Middle-earth, and bring him prisoner to Númenor. There Sauron encourages the men's desires for immortality; and the Kings of Númenor begin to worship Morgoth. Eventually those who were still faithful to the Valar leave for Middle-earth, while the followers of Morgoth and Sauron, led by King Ar-Pharazôn, launch a fleet against Valinor. As soon as they touch land, it is destroyed, as is the island of Númenor. At the Valar's request Ilúvatar reforms the physical world, and there remains no land connecting them with Middle-earth.

Finally in this volume there is an account of the Rings of Power and the Third Age. The surviving Númenoreans create the kingdom of Gondor, and they ally with the elves against Sauron, who has learnt the craft of ring-making from the Noldor, and is now wielder of the One Ring. In the end they defeat him in battle, and the Ring is cut from his hand. The rest of the story is familiar to readers of *The Lord of the Rings*, though it is told with a longer perspective. It recounts the story of the Ring from its forging to its destruction. Sauron's defeat means the end of all the Rings of Power, and most of the remaining elves leave; the Third Age draws to a close, and with it the history of Middle-earth.

This edition of *The Silmarillion* was only the start of Christopher Tolkien's editorial endeavours on his late father's behalf. In 1980 *Unfinished Tales of Númenor and Middle-Earth* was published, and this was followed by *The Book of Lost Tales parts 1 and 2*, and *The Lays of Beleriand*, which are currently to be found along with Christopher Tolkien's scholarly account of the development of *The Lord of The Rings*, *The Silmarillion* and other collected papers, in twelve volumes collectively entitled *The History Of Middle-Earth*. In each case J.R.R. Tolkien's papers are presented in chronological order with a scrupulous account of the changes which occurred from the first genesis of the stories during the 1914–18 war to the last versions of the early 1970s. These tales are often more expansive and lyrical than their counterparts in *The Silmarillion*. They include a great deal of poetry, much of which is of interest to students of the languages. But most of the tales are fragmentary, contradictory and almost always unfinished in some sense, and should only be read after the major published texts.

THE SHORT STORIES

A number of much shorter, more easily readable, stories were published during, and after, Tolkien's lifetime, which are not directly connected with the history of Middle-earth, but which give important insights into Tolkien's mind. They are all in some sense autobiographical.

Farmer Giles of Ham

Farmer Giles of Ham appeared in 1949. Farmer Giles uses his blunderbuss against a giant who is wandering in his fields and damaging his crops and livestock. The giant retreats, thinking he has been bitten by horseflies, and Farmer Giles becomes a local celebrity – so much so, that when the dragon Chrysophylax appears and begins to terrorize the neighbourhood, the King asks the farmer for help. Giles is reluctant to intervene, wisely being scared of the dragon, but eventually armed with Tailbiter, a dragonslayer's sword, he persuades Chrysophylax to share his hoard among the villagers, refuses to pay any to the King, and sets up his own little kingdom.

Leaf by Niggle

Leaf by Niggle appeared in 1945, and was republished in 1964 in *Tree and Leaf*, a short book which also contained the essay 'On Fairy Stories'; it is the only short work that doesn't seem to be aimed directly at children. Niggle is a little man who is quite good at painting, especially in matters of detail (he could paint leaves more effectively than trees), but not so good at helping his neighbour, Parish (partly because Parish doesn't like Niggle's paintings). Before Niggle can finish his life's project, a large painting of a tree against a countryside background, he has to go on a journey; and he lies inside a dark infirmary for a while before overheard voices allow him to continue his journey, commenting on his talent: 'He was a painter by nature. In a minor way, of course. Still, a Leaf by Niggle has a charm of its own' (*Tree and Leaf*, Allen and Unwin, 1964, p.27). Niggle comes to a countryside which he recognizes as his own painting, and he meets Parish again. They become firm friends before Niggle moves onwards in the company of a shepherd, while Parish waits for his wife to arrive.

Smith of Wootton Major

Smith of Wootton Major was first published in 1967, when Tolkien was at the height of his fame as an author. It was his last story, and it concerns a man who knows he is losing his powers, and who gives them

Leaf by Niggle.

up gracefully. At a village festival held every 24 years, 12 good children are invited to share a cake baked by the village's master cook. One year Alf, the apprentice cook, puts a star in the cake, which one of the children – Smith – swallows. This star allows Smith access to Faërie, and for many years he visits this world whenever he can, and sometimes meets the king and queen of the elves; he becomes a wise and gentle man. One day, on the way back from Faërie towards his family and ordinary life, he meets Alf, who is now the master cook. Alf tells him that he is leaving the village, and that it is time for Smith to pass his star on to a child of another generation. As Smith does so, carefully and wistfully choosing the child he thinks will benefit the most from this experience, he realizes that Alf the cook was in fact the elven king.

✴ ✴ ✴ *SUMMARY* ✴ ✴ ✴

Tolkien's fictional work can be seen as forming three related groups:

● *The Hobbit* and *The Lord of the Rings* connect his mythology with the modern world and orthodox storytelling.

● *The Silmarillion* and the other posthumous works explore the ways in which myth and history are constructed.

● The short stories provide contact between the author and the wider world of myth.

6 Tolkien's Other Work

This chapter looks at Tolkien's major academic works – which are an important part of his *oeuvre*. His editions of the medieval poems that he taught, and the few essays which can be found collected together in a volume called *The Monsters and the Critics and Other Essays*, help us to understand not only the literature that inspired him, but also how, and why, he wrote *The Silmarillion* and *The Lord of the Rings*. But in any case these essays are not dry exercises, which only make sense to a professional audience; they can be read with enjoyment by anyone who is interested in poetry, storytelling and language. Tolkien was a genuine philologist – he loved words, and he wrote about them with love.

A GREAT POEM

Before Tolkien published his essay 'The Monsters and the Critics' in 1936, *Beowulf,* a poem which was probably written in the eighth century, was seen as important because it was a document of the Anglo-Saxon language, and because it showed how far Christian concerns had appeared within Anglo-Saxon culture. In other words, scholars regarded it as an historical document rather than an important work of imaginative literature. This was partly because of its subject matter. A story of a hero defeating monsters seemed, to many early twentieth-century readers to be primitive. It is certainly about a world far removed from our own. The hall of a Danish king is raided by Grendel, a lake-dwelling monster who objects to the warriors' merrymaking. Grendel carries off and kills many of the king's finest warriors. Beowulf, a young leader of the Geats, arrives and after a struggle defeats and kills the ogre. Then the monster's mother appears, seeking revenge, and Beowulf descends to the bottom of the lake to destroy her as well. Beowulf returns to his own land, takes part in more orthodox wars against the Swedes, and becomes king. Fifty years later a great dragon lays waste to the land of the Geats. With the help of one trusted companion, Wiglaf, Beowulf destroys the dragon, but he is mortally wounded in the struggle, and the dying man passes on his kingdom to Wiglaf.

There was, Tolkien reported, general (if sometimes grudging) agreement that the poem was in some ways a fine achievement, written in, as he put it, 'highly-finished' verse. The chief problem for the critics was the monsters. Most literary critics were used to defending realism, and deriding fantasy literature, especially fantasy writing for adults. In the eighteenth century, Gothic novels such as Ann Radcliffe's *Mysteries of Udolpho* were dismissed as frightening tales for impressionable young women, and in the nineteenth century 'penny dreadfuls' such as Thomas Prescott Prest's *Varney the Vampire* were condemned as bloodthirsty adventure stories for equally impressionable young men. Ogres and dragons simply had no place in serious literature; they were for the entertainment of children. Therefore *Beowulf* could not be thought of as serious literature. Why did the poet not do as other authors of heroic writings did, and tell more of Beowulf's confrontations with other human beings?

Tolkien responded to the critics that this poem was not history, but literature. It contains an exquisite blend of two traditions: the heroic, legendary, Germanic (which could be called traditional Anglo-Saxon culture), and the Christian (which was a fairly recent import to Anglo-Saxon culture). The monsters are at the same time part of the legendary Anglo-Saxon past, and symbols of evil as seen through the eyes of a Christian. The first two monsters, Grendel and his mother, are said to be descendants of Cain, the first named murderer in the Bible; they are agents of Satan. The dragon, however, is 'a personification of malice, greed, destruction (the evil side of heroic life) and of the undiscriminating cruelty of fortune that distinguishes not good or bad (the evil aspect of all life)' (*The Monsters and the Critics*, Allen and Unwin, 1983, p.17). As a result, more than any confrontation between humans (who are enemies, but not necessarily evil), *Beowulf* shows us 'Man at war with the hostile world, and his inevitable overthrow in Time' (*The Monsters and the Critics*, Allen and Unwin, 1983, p.18). In other words, the poem explores key themes of *The Silmarillion* and *The Lord of the Rings*. Whatever *Beowulf* meant to literary critics in the 1930s, to Tolkien it was part of his view of the world, the world he was continually writing and re-writing from 1914 until his death in 1973. Through his essay on *Beowulf* we can see Tolkien's creative mind at work.

It is worth noting that Tolkien won the critical argument: *Beowulf*, along with the monsters, is now acknowledged to be a great poem. Seamus Heaney's translation of the poem won the Whitbread Prize 1999 (pushing the favourite, Joanne Rowling's *Harry Potter and the Prisoner of Azkaban*, into second place). But Tolkien has also won the argument because of the success of *The Hobbit* and *The Lord of the Rings*. Adult readers would see *Beowulf*'s tale of heroes, ogres and dragons – or indeed Harry Potter's encounters with the Dementors, and his shape-shifting godfather Sirius Black – very differently if *The Hobbit*, Tolkien's own tale of the defeat of a dragon, had not sold over thirty million copies worldwide. We read *Beowulf*, and the adventures of Harry Potter, through eyes which are informed by Tolkien's work and by the dungeons-and-dragons popular culture that he has inspired.

THE PUBLIC SCHOLAR

Tolkien's other very important academic work was the edition of the medieval poem *Sir Gawain and the Green Knight*, which he made with his Leeds University colleague E.V. Gordon in 1925. This long narrative poem is a story of temptation and the survival of Christian virtue and honour. At King Arthur's Court one Christmas a giant Green Knight arrives and challenges anyone to give him an axe-blow, which he will return in a year. Sir Gawain takes up the challenge, cutting the Knight's head off (as he rides away, severed head in hand, the head reminds Gawain of his promise). Gawain undertakes a long and dangerous journey to the Knight's land, where he stays at a castle. Three times Gawain is tempted by a lady, while her husband is out hunting. She wants to seduce him, but twice he only allows her to kiss him. On the third occasion he refuses her advances again, but she gives him a belt, saying it will protect him, and he wears it under his clothing when he encounters the Knight. The Knight's axe-blow grazes Gawain's neck; the Knight (who turns out to be the lady's husband) explains that if he had acknowledged the gift of the belt he would have been unhurt. Gawain returns to Court somewhat shamefaced, but he is praised for (more or less) maintaining his chastity.

Tolkien's edition of this medieval poem is an impressive achievement, which looks oddly familiar to the reader of *The Silmarillion* and *The Lord of the Rings*. The text is in a dialect that echoes some of the languages Tolkien uses in his later work (especially the language of the Rohirrim) and there are scholarly appendices which show painstaking attention to detail. Tolkien's edition demonstrates the extraordinary perfectionism of Tolkien the scholar – which is one reason why the promised editions of other medieval poems did not appear during his lifetime. Colleagues such as E.V. Gordon, Mary Salu or Simone d'Ardenne could sometimes persuade him to publish, even when Tolkien was convinced that there was more work to be done. Working by himself, he was never really satisfied, and like *The Silmarillion* and the other 'Lost Tales', his many introductions, glossaries, translations and indexes to the works he taught all his life remained unfinished (though many have been subsequently published). The *Letters* are full of promises to editors and publishers to send these texts by return of post; this seldom happened. Tolkien was a scholar and writer who would have remained in complete obscurity without the encouragement of colleagues like E.V. Gordon, friends such as C.S. Lewis, and publishers like Stanley and Rayner Unwin, and the edition of *Sir Gawain and the Green Knight* shows what he could have achieved given more time and self-confidence.

Sir Gawain and the Green Knight is also important, like *Beowulf*, as an influence on Tolkien's other work. Read it in a translation such as Tolkien's own, alongside the rest of the 1925 edition, and you will find that the poem demonstrates many of the connections between Tolkien's professional work and the languages and literature which he created in his spare time. The poem is written in the medieval dialect of the English Midlands – it is therefore connected with the Warwickshire of his childhood, which was the model for the Shire. The poem presents a version of the Quest story – the quest is Gawain's attempt to preserve the honour of Arthur's Court, even if he should die himself. It also presents a highly-qualified version of heroism – like Beowulf facing the dragon (and Frodo entering into Mordor), Gawain journeys to what he assumes will be his certain death; though, like Frodo, he is a flawed hero, because of his last-minute wearing of the hidden belt.

A SECRET VICE

It is probably less easy to see the influence of *Sir Gawain and the Green Knight* than *Beowulf* in Tolkien's work, however, because the last third of it is concerned with the defence of honour from sexual temptation, and Tolkien wrote so little about sexual behaviour. Predictably enough, when Tolkien publicly confessed to a secret vice, he was referring to his lifelong habit of creating languages. In 'A Secret Vice', another of the essays to be found in *The Monsters and the Critics,* he discusses the habit. As the title indicates, much of the tone of the discussion is self-mocking. He calls it a useless hobby, which takes time away from more useful activities such as time for family or employer (he was aware that some of his Oxford colleagues thought he was defrauding the public by spending his time on such activities rather than publishing academic essays). He even compares it at one point to opium addiction. However, in the end he defends his activity very strongly. He insists that all children have the ability and interest to make languages, but that it is driven from their minds along with other creative potential. What drives him, he tells us, is pleasure in the beauty of creation – the pleasures of making things fit together, the pleasures of calligraphy and the beauty of letters on the page, and of the sound of the words as they are spoken, the 'word-music' of the language, as he calls it. If the language itself is musical, he says, then anything spoken or written in it will be poetry. So the maker of languages is a craftsman, writer and composer all in one. He illustrates his argument with extracts from his own poetry, but he says nothing of the mythology. This is a defence of his lifelong fascination with language, but not of his own literature.

A Secret Vice.

THE STORY WRITER

'A Secret Vice' helps us to understand one half of Tolkien's preoccupations, and another of the essays in *The Monsters and The Critics*, 'On Fairy-Stories', helps us to understand the other half – his lifelong fascination with the literature of the fantastic. This is probably Tolkien's most important essay. It gives us insights into the ways in which he wanted to tell stories, and the emotional and psychological effects he wanted those stories to create. In this lecture, which was first delivered in Edinburgh in 1939, Tolkien was still at pains to defend a literature which seemed to have no place in the adult world. Again, he has won the argument, as far as the general public is concerned – though there are still many critics hostile to his work, as we will see in the next chapter.

First of all, Tolkien complains about the 'fairies' of the popular imagination – the ways in which fairies have been reduced to tiny creatures such as Tinker Bell in *Peter Pan*. For him fairies or elves are beings like ourselves in size who belong to a parallel world, Faërie, which is perilous for humans to enter, but important for them to imagine. Thinking of things which cannot or do not happen in our world, and making stories about them, he says, 'man becomes a sub-creator' (*The Monsters and the Critics*, Allen and Unwin, 1983, p.122). This is one of his most important ideas, and it is part of his Christian belief. Tolkien believed that human beings cannot really create anything new – certainly not creating life (primary creation); but they can explore the mysteries of creation by creating secondary worlds such as Faërie. By sub-creating they prove they are made by God: 'Fantasy remains a human right: we make in our measure and in our derivative mode, because we are made: and not only made, but made in the image and likeness of a Maker' (*The Monsters and the Critics*, Allen and Unwin, 1983, p.145).

Fantasy creates 'secondary worlds', which have an inner consistency but are not the same as the 'primary world' of observed fact. Seeing new worlds helps us to appreciate afresh the wonders of the world we actually live in – 'recovery', as Tolkien called it. But the new worlds also allow the reader to escape, which for Tolkien was a good thing. Escape from the world of factories, nine-to-five jobs and weapons of mass destruction into a world in which nature was more important, is important refreshment for the human spirit. In his words: 'A real taste for fairy stories was wakened by philology on the threshold of manhood, and quickened to full life by war' (*The Monsters and the Critics*, Allen and Unwin, 1983, p.135). Most importantly, therefore, we all desire escape from death; so the best fairy stories offer the supreme consolation of the unexpectedly happy ending. Tolkien invented his own word for this moment of surprising happiness – **eucatastrophe**, – which he said offered a glimpse of 'joy beyond the walls of the

KEYWORD

Eucastrophe: joins together Greek words for 'joy' and 'sudden event', so it literally means 'catastrophic pleasure'. For Tolkien, certain stories offered moments of magical joy beyond hope – a princess awoken from years of sleep by a kiss, for example.

world' (The Monster and the Critics, Allen and Unwin, 1983, p.153). *The Lord of the Rings* offers several such moments of eucatastrophe. The Riders of Rohan arrive on the battlefield of the Pelennor outside Minas Tirith, their horns blowing wildly, the grass shining under their horses' hooves as the darkness lifts; and the chief of the Nazgûl is defeated. After the Ring is destroyed, the Fellowship meets once more on the field of Cormallen. Frodo and Sam cry with joy as the poet sings their own story, which they had tried to imagine would happen as they approached Mordor. Frodo glimpses that joy once more as he approaches the Western shore; the veils of Middle-earth are withdrawn and he sees the world anew. Dying from this world, he escapes into the next.

✷ ✷ ✷SUMMARY✷ ✷ ✷

Read the essays and other scholarly work because they help understand:

- Tolkien's fascination with languages.

- his principal sources.

- his attempt to make a 'new mythology'.

- his belief in the power of story-telling.

7 The Master and the Critics

> J.R.R. Tolkien's chief contribution to the literature of the 20th century was to ignore it almost completely. He wrote ... to retrieve something that the discordance of the modern age seemed intrinsically to threaten – the old, secure, prepubertal moral certainties of late-Edwardian England.
>
> (Andrew Rissik, 'Middle Earth, Middlebrow',
> *The Guardian*, 2 November 2000)

This is a typical response to Tolkien from the United Kingdom's literary establishment of academics and journalists. By and large, academic literary criticism has ignored contemporary fantasy literature, and most of those critics who have referred to Tolkien's work have been negative about it. There seems to be no single or simple explanation for this. There is, however, a growing minority who defend his work against the negative views. This chapter will try to act as a guide to these arguments (but not to prove Tolkien innocent or guilty: it is for those who read his work to make up their own minds).

Tolkien's critical reputation was always higher in the USA. Although there were some negative responses, *The Lord of the Rings* was taken seriously in academic criticism as well as popular culture, almost from its initial publication, though the public debate about the unauthorized paperback version of *The Lord of the Rings* undoubtedly stimulated sales in the mid-1960s, and this led to an increase in academic interest. The university system in the USA continues to provide more opportunities for scholars to research and write about Tolkien, and many influential Tolkien scholars – Jane Chance, for example – are American.

REALISM AND MODERNISM

Negative criticism of Tolkien's writing can be reduced to a few basic positions. Firstly he does not fit with contemporary literature, since he is neither a realist nor a **modernist**. In this view, as with the criticism of *Beowulf* that Tolkien referred to in 1936, there is no place for fantasy literature for adults in the modern world. Realism was the most important form of fiction in the nineteenth century, and most twentieth-century novels were also realist in nature. Places, times and characters are described just as if they could have happened to the reader. Novels are usually written from the viewpoint of a neutral observer – Charles Dickens's *Little Dorrit*, for example – or in the first person as if they were autobiography, such as Dickens's *Great Expectations*. This type of fiction did not usually represent heroism – in Thackeray's *Vanity Fair*, the setting is the early nineteenth century, but the great battles of the Napoleonic wars (which were happening at the time, and were vitally important to Britain and the rest of Europe) are hardly mentioned. *Vanity Fair* is even subtitled *A Novel Without a Hero*. The main plot of most realist fiction was, in the nineteenth-century novel at least, centred on a romance between a man and a woman, and generally led to marriage. 'Reader, I married him', is the fairly typical opening sentence of the final chapter of Charlotte Brontë's *Jane Eyre*.

> **KEYWORD**
>
> Modernism: a movement which started in the early twentieth century. Writers, artists and musicians broke with the conventions of their art forms, producing work which was difficult to understand. It often shocked and disturbed audiences.

Modernism disrupted many of these literary conventions. In particular, modernist writers tried to find ways of getting inside the minds of characters, showing the reader what they were thinking as well as what they did. Virginia Woolf, for instance, developed 'stream of consciousness', a way of writing that tries to show the connected thought inside a character's head, rather than the more orderly form of reported speech. The results were often shocking, displaying people's confusions, desires and hatreds. But as well as trying in this way to 'improve' on realism by looking at real peoples' real thought, modernist writers were more aware that they were writing 'literature', not 'the truth' about the characters who they imagined. Literature began to deal with itself, and not to engage so directly with the outside world. James Joyce's *Ulysses*, for example, is a very complex re-imagining of Homer's epic poem *The Odyssey*, all packed into a day in the life of an ordinary Dubliner. Modernists played games with the conventions of form, including the third-person and first-person narrative mode. The narrator became less reliable – after all, how could an observer really know other peoples' thoughts? However, novelists (including Joyce) did not simply abandon the 'real'; they dealt with other experiences. Their stories were less centred on marriage; they began to explore other kinds of sexual desire, and the motivations for the darker side of human activities such as murder. And once again there was no hero – modernist literature was far more likely to portray an anti-hero or anti-heroine, someone who was deeply flawed and a failure in life, as the central figure of their text.

Tolkien's work does not easily fit either pattern. It is not realist – it is not about the present or recent past, and it is not about a recognizably real world such as Dickens's London, even though much of it is written as if it were real history and geography. Neither can it easily be called modernist. The new mythology of *The Silmarillion*, though it is undoubtedly an experiment with literary form, makes little attempt to analyse the complex desires and motives of the characters, or (despite the many different versions of the stories) to suggest that there might be more than one way to look at a person or event.

We simply have to take it as read, for example, that the characters Tolkien calls 'evil' really are just that. This is partly because he almost always writes about the 'good'. Neither Morgoth nor Sauron are allowed to say much in their own defence, and the stories never represent their viewpoints. In *The Lord of the Rings*, Sauron's speech is very occasionally reported, and his motives are guessed at by his opponents. Saruman is eventually allowed to speak – but we first hear his speech, too, as reported by Gandalf, and we only actually encounter him speaking for himself after he has been defeated, when he seems to be almost a pantomime baddie. The orcs speak, but only insipid words of hate and envy, despite (we assume, as Tolkien provides few details) having a history and culture of their own which goes back for tens of thousands of years. Even their languages are less well represented than those of the 'good' characters. The only time we encounter more than a few words of the 'black language' of Mordor, for example, is in Gandalf's rendition of the Ring's binding spell. Therefore, to some readers, *The Lord of the Rings* and especially *The Silmarillion* seem to be simple morality tales, the kind of story that the realist novel had replaced. For all these reasons Tolkien's work seems to belong to the Middle Ages, like the literature which he taught – it is anachronistic, written in the wrong place at the wrong time.

THE WRONG TYPE OF FANTASY?

A second type of critique is offered by people who approve of fantasy literature but who think that Tolkien's work is insufficiently sophisticated as fantasy. In a series of works on fantasy literature, Colin Manlove has consistently represented Tolkien as an important writer. However, his longest treatment of *The Lord of the Rings* is highly critical of its presentation of evil. As Manlove points out in *Modern Fantasy. Five Studies*, most of the good characters in *The Lord of the Rings* survive. This suggests that we have here a simple morality tale (telling us to be good, do the right thing, and you will be rewarded with long life and happiness) rather than a genuine exploration of the problem of good and evil.

Manlove accuses Tolkien of cheating in his presentation of evil. Since we never meet Sauron face to face or hear his words, the greatest evil present in the book is the symbolic power of the One Ring, which was made to draw all to the darkness and bind them. In other words, the Ring should corrupt all who wear it. To an extent it does. It slips from Isildur's finger, and he is killed; it turns Gollum into a wicked creature in his own small way; it stretches Bilbo's life into weariness and begins to warp his mind; the thought of possessing it terrifies Gandalf and Galadriel (though both have strong fantasies about having and using it); and it breaks Boromir's mind. But when Frodo uses it the Ring does not betray him, and instead leads him to meet Aragorn, and later to escape from the Company. After the Weathertop attack he does not show himself to Sauron's forces through wearing the Ring. Neither does Sam, who takes it from Frodo on the edge of Mordor – and can then hand it back without much regret when Frodo asks for it. Gollum, meanwhile, betrays Frodo to Shelob; but he does not simply murder Frodo and take the Ring, despite his constant mutterings, and several opportunities to do so when the hobbits are asleep and he knows the Ring is inches from his grasp. Finally, Manlove insists, the Ring is compromised because it does not destroy Frodo. Gandalf tells Frodo early in the story that giving up the Ring would break his mind. But it does not. When the Ring is finally bitten from Frodo's hand, he does not collapse or have a nervous breakdown. This is hardly a ring of absolute power. Therefore, argues Manlove, Tolkien cheats us. He does not present absolute evil. This is an adventure story in which the good have the odds loaded in their favour.

A similar concern was behind the criticisms offered by Edwin Muir, who reviewed the trilogy as it was being published in the 1950s. These early reviews, alongside one by Edmund Wilson, set the standards for hostile critics, who have been repeating these points ever since – similar positions were taken in 2002 by the Scottish academic Tom Nairn, as well as Andrew Rissik's article written in 2000 which was quoted at the start of this chapter. Muir (who said he was not an opponent of fantasy as such, and liked some aspects of the book, the ents in particular) claimed that *The Lord of the Rings* was a story for male juveniles masquerading as a book for adults; in fact, he said, it was just a very long version of the adventure story, of the type which was to be found in the *Boy's Own* paper. The hobbits were actually teenage boys, playing around in an adult world. The worst offence, according to Muir, was that there were no real women in the book; Arwen, Galadriel, and the rest were male adolescent fantasy figures (*The Observer*).

While this was a slightly odd accusation to make even in the 1950s (then, as now, adolescent boys have strong sexual feelings, and there is nothing remotely sexual, let alone pornographic, in figures such as Arwen) there is a great deal of evidence to support Muir's accusation. Many of the spin-offs from the world of Middle-earth into popular culture – the *Warhammer* board games, the heroic adventure games for computers, and many of the various versions of dungeons and dragons, are almost entirely masculine, featuring male characters (or females who really are adolescent boys' fantasy figures, with exaggerated breasts and hips – an obvious computer-game example being the heroic archaeologist Lara Croft). Such games are played in the main by teenage boys, and older men who see no point in growing up.

The Peter Jackson film series seems to acknowledge this critique and respond to it, representing women more prominently than the book. For example, the first Jackson film substitutes Arwen for Glorfindel as the elf who meets the company after Frodo has been attacked on Weathertop. She then rescues Frodo by riding with him to Rivendell, rather than merely putting him on a horse and telling the horse to run fast, as Glorfindel does in the book. However, the film can also be seen as a more 'masculine' product than the book – it is certainly much better at showing violent adventures than the more subtle linguistic and cultural contrasts that are there in the written story. There is little or no use of the book's oral culture (the poetry and stories the characters use to establish their identity). Instead the film substitutes aggressive clichés of species difference, such as Gimli's assertive cry 'no-one tosses a dwarf!' *The Fellowship of the Ring's* least violent powerful male figure, Tom Bombadil (who rescues the hobbits from Old Man Willow with a cheerful song rather than a sword-thrust), does not appear in the film. By contrast, the sequence in Moria is dominated by the fight with the cave troll, which is a highly exaggerated version of the book's brief encounter (in the book, the narrative of the dwarves' failure in Moria is at least as important as the subsequent fight.).

TOLKIEN THE CONSERVATIVE?

The inadequate representation of women through stereotypes of beauty, purity and wisdom, and the equally dubious association of masculinity, power and violence, is one aspect of the feminist critique of Tolkien. Rosemary Jackson (later echoed by Germaine Greer, among other **feminist critics**) proposes that Tolkien is deeply conservative. Jackson's influential book *Fantasy. The Literature of Subversion* claims that the object of fantasy literature must be to present an alternative to the existing social order: to present a different world in which men and women, and people of different races, live more fulfilled lives without oppressing each other. Some forms of science fiction try to do this, but Tolkien's fantasy does not. It shows us a world structured by aristocratic male power which is enforced by violence.

KEYWORD

Feminist criticsim: questions prejudices parading themselves as truths about the nature of femininity, and seeks to revalue the work of women writers, which has been historically undervalued in a male-dominated literary profession.

Middle-earth is indeed a war-dominated world in which the violent actions of men achieve power or transmit it to other men, while women and children are often passive victims. Again this is more true of *The Lord of the Rings* (and especially *The Hobbit*) than *The Silmarillion*. In *The Silmarillion* the Valar are differentiated by gender identity rather than biology, but Yavanna is among the most powerful of the Valar. She gives Middle-earth its first natural environment and its first sources of light (the Two Trees of Valinor). The few powerful female characters in *The Lord of the Rings* are underdeveloped as actors in the drama – this is especially notable in the relatively passive, resigned Galadriel, who could have been a leading light in the Council at Rivendell, and who could have been chosen to be a member of the Fellowship but chose to stay in Lothlórien, where she provides material assistance to the men. *The Lord of the Rings* also features Éowyn, who it seems wants to go to war partly as a form of therapy for her sexual frustration (she desires Aragorn). She is a successful warrior who kills the chief Nazgûl. She is then, however, persuaded into a more pacific and passive womanhood (and into marriage) by Faramir, while they rest together in the Houses of Healing:

> 'I stand in Minas Anor, the Tower of the Sun', she said, 'and behold! The Shadow has departed! I will be a shieldmaiden no more, nor vie with the great Riders, nor seek joy only in the songs of slaying. I will be a healer, and love all things that grow and are not barren.' (Book VI, Chapter 5)

Connected to this critique about gender issues is a broader argument that Tolkien's work is socially and politically conservative – sexist, class-bound and racist. Once more there is a strong case for the critics. *The Silmarillion, The Hobbit* and *The Lord of the Rings* are all **patrilineal.** From Aragorn son of Arathorn to Frodo son of Drogo, all the principal species – elves, dwarves, men and hobbits – identify themselves through their fathers' names as well as their own. Of the principal male characters only Gandalf does not reveal his family history

KEYWORD

Patrilineal: inheritance through the father's line.

in this way. This patrilineal system is also a class system – families are structured round the legal right of inheritance, and not everyone inherits rank, wealth or ability. For Tolkien rank and wealth, like outstanding ability, are good things. 'Noble' is used throughout Tolkien's work as a term of approval. Kings are natural leaders. Théoden, dying, announces that he is going to the hall of his fathers, where they will receive him as an equal thanks to his great deeds on the battlefield that day. Figures like Aragorn (the descendent of Isildur, who had cut the Ring from the hand of Sauron), Faramir (descendant of the long line of Stewards of Gondor) and Éomer, King Théoden's sister's son, all embody the basic principle of an aristocracy, which is that a talent for leadership can (and should) be inherited. In the absence of such a King, the state and the people are damaged: the dwarves await the return of Durin, who they believe will restore their greatness in Moria. The Return of the King to Gondor is the return of a natural order, in which biology is destiny.

However, it is worth remembering that hobbits represent Tolkien's version of the modern world, and that although hobbits, like the other species, are patrilineal (and fond of tracing their family trees), there is no aristocratic system in the Shire itself. There are rich and less rich hobbits, and there are prominent families, but there is no inherited political or military leadership. The Shire as we see it in *The Hobbit* and at the beginning of *Lord of the Rings* is a peaceful political **anarchy**, with an entirely symbolic mayor, and public services dominated by a postal service. On the other hand, in the Shire as elsewhere the 'working class' is seen as less intellectually and morally capable than the richer folk. Critics on the left dislike this contrast of aristocratic heroes, deserving rich,

> **KEYWORD**
>
> Anarchy: a society in which there is no ruling power (such as a monarchy or a parliament) and in which each individual has absolute freedom.

and ignorant working class villains. Ted Sandyman is a fool who enthusiastically supports industrialization even though it destroys his independence (his father was the mill-owner), and makes him into a worker. Sam Gamgee is portrayed as a loyal servant, constantly deferring to 'the master' with dog-like devotion (however, he becomes a leader in the Shire, and he even helps to write the book). Elsewhere in Middle-earth we seldom meet ordinary people and when we do they accept the social hierarchies they are born into. Beregond, the soldier of Gondor who befriends Pippin, is honest and dutiful, as is the wordy nurse Ioreth. Haldir, who guides the Fellowship around Lothlórien, is an ordinary elf who acknowledges Celeborn and Galadriel's superiority. But on the whole we meet and hear the important – princes among elves such as Gildor and Galadriel, dwarves from important families, the chief and oldest ent, and even Shagrat and Gorbag, the leading orcs from Minas Morgul and Cirith Ungol.

The orcs as a whole, meanwhile, whether bosses or footsoldiers, are a caricature of the industrial working class, energetic and aggressive, full of hate for each other and their employers, as well as the enemies they are supposed to be fighting, and lacking many of the basics of culture. 'Class', in other words, is also represented through 'race'. Tolkien's races or species are arranged in a very obvious hierarchy. At the top there are the angelic Valar and Maiar. On Middle-earth itself the wise, beautiful elves are at the top and the hideous and hate-filled orcs at the bottom. In the middle are the various groups of men, and they too are ordered in a hierarchy of goodness from the almost-elvish Númenoreans, and their golden-haired allies the Rohirrim, to the Haradrim who ally with Sauron.

One aspect of these rankings of species should be noted. Tolkien consistently uses white and black as **metaphors** for good and bad. Tolkien claimed that hatred of apartheid was in his bones, and it is true that *The Hobbit*, *The Lord of the Rings* and *The Silmarillion* are all concerned with the ways in which, despite their differences, elves, dwarves, (some) men, ents and hobbits combine against orcs, wargs, balrogs, (some) men and the other species that act for Morgoth and Sauron. Nonetheless, the free peoples are almost always presented as white – with the exception of the Stoors, hobbits who live in the East of the Shire, who are said to be 'browner of skin' than the inhabitants of Hobbiton – and many of their opponents, such as the Haradrim, are 'swart' or dark-skinned. We have a life's work, which can be read as extolling the virtues of whiteness, though it is unlikely that Tolkien would have used these metaphors so freely were he writing today (similarly he would probably not have been so positive about the virtues of tobacco smoke).

> **KEYWORD**
>
> Metaphor: a form of comparison using a word or idea that is not literally applicable to what the writer is describing, in order to illustrate shared characteristics.

All these arguments about Tolkien the conservative were repeated in the critics' response to the Waterstone's poll (1999) in which *The Lord of the Rings* was voted best book of the twentieth century. Its rivals in the top ten included the modernist classic *Ulysses*, by James Joyce, and more contemporary fantasies such as William Golding's *Lord of the Flies* and Orwell's *1984*. Despite this triumph, Tolkien's critics continued to represent him as an anachronistic conservative failure, and their voices are still prominent in the literary press: Germaine Greer's response to the Waterstone's poll, for example, was that Tolkien's success represented her worst nightmare. However, in the last fifteen years, several critics, including a few based in the UK, have written seriously in Tolkien's defence.

IN DEFENCE OF FANTASY

The most comprehensive recent defence of Tolkien is *J.R.R. Tolkien: Author of the Century* by Tom Shippey, a former Professor of English at Leeds University, indeed a philologist in Tolkien's footsteps. In a central chapter Shippey deals with the problem of evil in *The Lord of the Rings*. Tolkien was one of a number of twentieth-century authors (including Lewis, Golding, Orwell and Kurt Vonnegut), who experienced the horrors of mechanized mass warfare, and his sense of the reality of evil, and the need for a mythology to explain the occurrence of evil, is based on these experiences. Shippey defends *The Lord of the Rings* against Colin Manlove's accusations. The nature of evil, according to Shippey, is deliberately left ambivalent. It is embodied in the 'wraith', the insubstantial, shadowy figure of fear which is *itself* the product of corruption and fear, represented primarily by the Nazgûl. Saruman becomes a wraith 'partly by merging himself with his own cause, discarding any sense of means in pursuit of some increasingly impossible end, and partly by the self-deceptions of language' (T. Shippey, *J.R.R. Tolkien: Author of the Century*, p.127); it is as a wraith that he dies, his shadow dissolving before a wind from the West. Shippey shows how Tolkien makes use of this insubstantial sign of evil to ask what it is, and where if, at all, lie our responsibilities for it. Is evil merely the absence of good; is it inaction on our part? The choice not to destroy the Ring but to hide it would have been as evil as one to use it. So evil could be simply the result of our own choices, or it could be an absolute quality that only some creatures and actions have, or it could be we do not know, but we are invited to choose; Tolkien presents all three as possibilities. Time and again we are told that Frodo is 'tempted' to put on the Ring; and that he is also, at the same time, 'commanded' to do so. Sam, too, is both 'tempted' by the inner vision of the heroic Samwise the Strong, and feels that he is being willed to put the Ring on by some outside force. Evil is undoubtedly present throughout the book, but whether from within or without it is for the reader to decide.

THE CHRISTIAN VIEW

For some critics, including many from the USA, the solution is clear. Tolkien was a lifelong, deeply-committed Catholic, and all of his work (including his views of good and evil) is therefore Christian in nature. Again there is plenty of evidence for this view. The Bible is among the fundamental sources for Tolkien's mythology. The opening of *The Silmarillion* is a version of the Old Testament's creation story, and the subsequent stories of the First and Second Ages deal with the relationships between elves, men and good and fallen angels. The language of both *The Silmarillion* and *The Lord of the Rings* (especially the final volume, *The Return of the King*) owe a great deal to the Standard Authorized version of the Bible. Tolkien connected the Christian story with fantasy literature in the essay 'On Fairy Stories' – at the end of the essay he comments that the Gospels are the ultimate eucatastrophe. For him the story of the crucifixion and resurrection of Jesus Christ reveals precisely that surprisingly happy ending which defeats death, the 'joy beyond the confines of the world', which Tolkien wanted to achieve as a storyteller. Both Frodo and Gandalf can be seen as Christ-like figures; perhaps Gandalf is the closer. He seems to die; on his return he reveals that he has 'been sent back, for a time', in the same way that Christ briefly returned to earth before the Ascension. Also, like Christ on his return to life after the Resurrection, he is physically different – Gandalf the White, now able to command Saruman and lead the opponents of Mordor in battle.

Aragorn can also be seen as a Christ-like figure, as Kurt Bruner and Jim Ware point out in their short book *Finding God in The Lord of the Rings*. They go through the story (and parts of *The Silmarillion* and *The Hobbit*) commenting on the closeness of the story to the Christian message. Discussing Aragorn's coronation, they write:

> The power of this scene lies in its appeal to something deep within the psyche of every reader: the wish for a King who is truly worthy of loyalty and worship. When he rises with the crown upon his head, Aragorn is revealed to be just such a king … As such, he cannot fail to remind us of Jesus, once the humble carpenter of Nazareth, now the rider of the white horse, the Word of God, whose name is Faithful and True.
>
> (K. Bruner and J. Ware, *Finding God in The Lord of the Rings*, p.97)

There is no representation of Christianity itself in Tolkien's major works. There is very little organized religion in of any sort in the stories. When it does appear it is wrong – as with the Númenoreans' worship of Morgoth, before they try to attack Valinor. However, as Christopher Tolkien points out, many of the older stories in the mythology hint that the Valar are interfering on earth, and in the hobbit stories there is often a sense of a higher purpose or controlling will, which could be identified as God. Gandalf says to Bilbo in *The Hobbit*: 'you don't really suppose, do you, that all your adventures and escapes were managed by mere luck, just for your sole benefit?' (*The Hobbit*, Chapter 19). Similarly Gandalf tells Frodo in *The Lord of the Rings* 'there was something else at work, beyond any design of the Ring-maker. I can put it no plainer than by saying that Bilbo was meant to find the Ring, and not by its maker. In which case you also were meant to have it' (*Lord of the Rings* Book I, Chapter 2).

For Tom Shippey, however, despite such evidence *The Lord of the Rings* is not the Catholic work that Tolkien himself claimed it to be. Instead Shippey proposes that it deals with the world in which Tolkien found himself – a world without any sense of God's command (the Christian faith was declining rapidly in Britain). The elves, for all their connections with the Valar, and their hard-won ability to see the consequences of their actions (which means that they are able to foretell the future with some skill), are living in a world without divine revelation: they do not know that they will be 'saved'. In a sense Tolkien's 'new mythology' was an unacknowledged substitute for Christianity. Whether or not it was Tolkien's intention, it has become an active substitute for other faiths in the minds of many of its most enthusiastic readers.

READERS AS CRITICS

New technology, especially the growth of the worldwide web, has empowered different kinds of criticism and allowed fan cultures to flower in new ways. The voluntary (and unpaid) reviews to be found on the book-selling website www.Amazon.com, for instance, offer the perspective of a very different reading public from the professional writers who normally write reviews for newspapers and magazines. Furthermore, many of the thousands of websites devoted to Tolkien's work carry not just uncritical fan worship (though there is a great deal of that), but serious debates about the moral, religious and philosophical content of the works. Some of this was brought together when the Peter Jackson film sequence was in production. The producers of the movie interacted with the enormous web-based community of Tolkien fans, and some aspects of the film were changed as a result of this dialogue. In this world of fan-consumers, we need professional critics less.

TOLKIEN THE RADICAL?

There is an enormous global community of Tolkien fans, and many of them are drawn together by the worldwide web. Patrick Curry, in *Defending Middle-Earth*, emphasizes Tolkien's own insistence on community as one of the radical lessons to be drawn from his work. In the mechanized modern age, Curry argues, community is under threat, by individualism as much as by machines. Furthermore his insistence on community based on the balanced use of the natural world, makes him a radical, not a conservative.

Readers of Tolkien were drawing lessons about environmental politics long before his academic readers began to notice such issues. They continue to do so now: there is growing interest in 'ecological criticism', and this is one way in which Tolkien's work will enter the 'canon' of approved literary texts. Critics such as Jonathan Bate have argued that there is an important tradition of writing about environmental issues within English literature, from Wordsworth and William Blake early in the nineteenth century, to John Ruskin and William Morris (who was a direct influence on Tolkien) at the end of the nineteenth century, and in the twentieth century the work of Ted Hughes and John Fowles. It is easy to see how Tolkien can be read as an ecological thinker. His detailed descriptions of landscapes, his obvious joy in the beauty of trees, his invention of their herds, the ents, and above all his angry opposition to the depravations of industrialization and urbanization, mark Tolkien out as a pioneer in the literature of environmental awareness.

Awareness of this literary tradition proposes that we read Tolkien in a very different way – which (as Curry says) makes him politically positive. Radical environmentalism is a 'conservatism' of a sort – its followers want to preserve the world as it is rather than change it for the worse – but it is equally politically radical in a world that values capital growth before the interests of any living thing. This form of criticism is beginning to return Tolkien to his readers, acknowledging that their reading of his work always was important.

* * *SUMMARY* * *

Some critics have accused Tolkien of writing:

• anachronistic work, which has no place in the modern world.

• masculine adventure stories with no place for positive female characters.

• reactionary portrayals of working class characters.

• racist depictions of the different species, with whites seen as best.

Others have responded by praising Tolkien's:

• immense skill as a narrative story teller.

• ability to confront the problem of evil.

• positive portrayal of alliances among species.

• importance as an ecological writer.

Read all the work, and make your own mind up.

8 Where to Next?

READ TOLKIEN'S WORK

Read it several times. As you will have realized by now, the essays and editions, the stories and poems, the mythologies and maps are all part of a connected life's work. As you read and re-read them you will understand the unfolding connections, and the more you know the more you will get from the long and short stories. For those who do not have the time to read, but can listen, there is a great deal of material in various audio formats, including the BBC's adaptations of *The Hobbit* and *The Lord of the Rings,* and complete audiobooks of *The Lord of the Rings* and *The Silmarillion.* You should also see Peter Jackson's movies – but only when you have read the book!

READ TOLKIEN'S SOURCES

Most of the texts which inspired Tolkien are available in translation, including Tolkien's own translation of *Sir Gawain and the Green Knight,* and Seamus Heaney's prize-winning version of *Beowulf.* Editions of Sir Thomas Malory's *The Morte d'Arthur,* the *Mabinogion,* the Icelandic *Sagas,* and *The Kalevala* are listed under Further Reading.

READ THE EXPERTS

The best biography is still Humphrey Carpenter's *J.R.R. Tolkien. A Biography,* which has a good bibliography of Tolkien's writings. Carpenter went on to edit *The Letters of J.R.R. Tolkien.* These two books will give you a good idea of Tolkien's developing ideas, and you should read them before you tackle Christopher Tolkien's massive *The History of Middle-Earth,* which will give all the background you are likely to need on J.R.R. Tolkien's major works.

Criticism of Tolkien as a fantasy writer can be found (briefly) in Rosemary Jackson, *Fantasy,* and in Colin Manlove, *Modern Fantasy.*

Five Studies. Manlove's recent *The Fantasy Literature of England* is more sympathetic to Tolkien. The best of the recent defences of Tolkien's work are Patrick Curry, *Defending Middle-Earth,* and Tom Shippey, *J.R.R. Tolkien: Author of the Century.* If you are interested in academic work about Tolkien, start with Shippey, or Jane Chance, *Tolkien's Art: a Mythology for England.* Kurt Bruner and Jim Ware's *Finding God in The Lord of the Rings* is a brief and enthusiastic example of Christian criticism. For the emerging field of ecological criticism, try Jonathan Bate and Leonard Coupe *The Green Studies Reader. From Romanticism to Ecocriticism.*

READ TOLKIEN'S CONTEMPORARIES

Tolkien was not alone in examining mythology. During the early twentieth century the legendary past was used by others for a number of similar purposes. There was a massive upsurge of interest in the boundary between history and myth, including Jessie L. Weston's *From Ritual to Romance* (Cambridge University Press, 1920); Sir James Frazer's *The Golden Bough* (Macmillan, 1922); and Robert Graves's *The White Goddess* (Faber, 1948). All three books (in very different ways) explored the ways in which magic and myth were used in the past, and all seemed to suggest that the same myths and stories were still in use in the present.

It worried Tolkien that the most prominent British strand in this reinvention of the past was Celtic – as it remains to this day. Examples include novels such as John Cowper Powys's *A Glastonbury Romance* (John Lane, 1933), T.H. White's *The Once and Future King* (Collins, 1958), Mary Stewart's *Crystal Cave* (Hodder & Stoughton, 1970), trilogy, and Marion Bradley's *The Mists of Avalon* (Knopf, 1982). Even T.S. Eliot's modernist poem *The Waste Land* (Hogarth, 1923) uses the Fisher King, a character from the quest for the Holy Grail (which is part of the Arthurian cycle). C.S. Lewis's novel *That Hideous Strength* (*Bodley Head,* 1945), which is a hostile response to *The Waste Land,* also uses the Fisher King, and in Lewis's story Arthur's wizard Merlin is revived in order to lead the fight against the powers of ultimate evil that threaten the earth. Only E.R. Eddison's *The Worm Ouroboros* (Jonathan Cape, 1922) was comparatively free of reliance on these older stories, as was the later *Gormenghast* (Eyre and Spottiswoode, 1950) fantasy by Mervyn Peake.

READ RECENT FANTASY WRITERS
Your local bookshop will have many examples of contemporary fantasy. However, many authors who have written fantasy since Tolkien are still in his shadow. None can match his invention of languages and long histories, although many of them are worth reading in their own right. Terry Pratchett is among the best of the post-Tolkien (rather than copy-Tolkien) fantasy writers, and his work, like Tolkien's, can also be found in popular cultural forms such as online Internet games. The recent success of J.K. Rowling and Philip Pullman has led to the publication of a wave of new children's fantasy writers, such as Lemony Snicket; the work of Ursula le Guin and Alan Garner (each of whom write for adults and children) is also recommended.

JOIN THE TOLKIEN SOCIETY
If you are or become a Tolkien fan, The Tolkien Society will foster your enthusiasm. For more information write to:
    The Membership Secretary
    The Tolkien Society
    56 Wentworth Crescent
    Ash Vale
    Surrey GU12 5LF
    United Kingdom.
    You can also join online at http://www.tolkiensociety.org

This brings us to the worldwide web…

TOLKIEN ON THE INTERNET
The Internet is home to a massive community of Tolkien enthusiasts and commentators; there are literally hundreds of thousands of Tolkien-related websites. You could spend a lifetime hopping between

these sites, looking at maps and illustrations, reading posts on notice boards or longer pieces of writing which range from long, short, serious, comic and even pornographic **fanfics,** to sober discussions about the role of the Valar.

The Peter Jackson films have an official website (which was the most-hit site of the year 2001), which has links to the rest of the fan community, at http://www.lordoftherings.net.

KEYWORD

Fanfic: literally fiction writers by a fan. Fans use the characters from the books, television series or films, which they like, add their own stories, and publish them in fanzines or on the Internet.

For Tolkien matters in general, a good unofficial site – also with movie information but a lot more besides – is http://www.theonering.net.

This is as good an entry as any into the vast maze of Tolkien websites. Happy surfing!

Chronology of Major Works

1892	Tolkien born in Bloemfontein, South Africa
1925	with E.V.Gordon, *Sir Gawain and the Green Knight*
1937	'Beowulf: the Monsters and the Critics' appears in *Proceedings of the British Academy*. Reprinted in the 1983 collection of essays *The Monsters and the Critics*
1937	*The Hobbit*
1945	*Leaf by Niggle* appears in *The Dublin Review*. Reprinted in *Tree and Leaf*
1947	'On Fairy Stories' appears in *Essays Presented to Charles Williams*. Reprinted in *Tree and Leaf* and in the 1983 collection of essays *The Monsters and the Critics*
1949	*Farmer Giles of Ham*
1954–5	*The Lord of the Rings* appears in three volumes
1962	*The Adventures of Tom Bombadil*, a brief collection of poems
1964	*Tree and Leaf*
1967	*Smith of Wootton Major*
1973	Tolkien dies in Bournemouth. All work after this is edited by Christopher Tolkien
1977	*The Silmarillion*
1980	*Unfinished Tales*
1983	*The Monsters and the Critics and Other Essays*
1983–96	*The History of Middle Earth*, in twelve volumes, including *The Book of Lost Tales volumes 1 and 2*, and *The Lays of Beleriand*

GLOSSARY

Alliteration A sequence of words with the same letter or sound.

Anachronism Something which seems to be in the wrong time – a horse and cart on a motorway, for example.

Anarchy A society in which there is no ruling power (such as a monarchy or a parliament) and in which each individual has absolute freedom.

Archaic Characteristic of a much earlier period – in Tolkien's case this means using old-fashioned words and grammar. See also **anachronism**.

Aristocracy A ruling group which transmits its power by inheritance.

Ecology The balance of the natural world, including the lives and deaths of all living things.

Eucatastrophe Joins together Greek words for 'joy' and 'sudden event', so it literally means 'catastrophic pleasure'. For Tolkien, certain stories offered moments of magical joy beyond hope – a princess awoken from years of sleep by a kiss, for example.

Fall The Biblical story of the entry of evil into the world. Satan persuades Eve to taste the forbidden fruit. She then persuades Adam to taste it, and as a result the couple are banished from Paradise.

Fanfic Literally fiction written by a fan. Fans use the characters from the books, television series or films which they like, add their own stories, and publish them in fanzines or on the Internet.

Feminist criticism Questions prejudices parading themselves as truths about the nature of femininity, and seeks to revalue the work of women writers, which has been historically undervalued in a male-dominated literary profession.

Feudalism A relationship in which the owner of the land grants the use of it to an inferior in return for favours such as military service. Such relationships were common in medieval Europe.

Linguistics The term usually used now for the scientific study of languages. Professional linguistics is less interested in the historical evolution of languages than in what they mean now, and it uses speech for evidence rather more than literature.

Metaphor A form of comparison using a word or idea that is not literally applicable to what the writer is describing, in order to illustrate shared characteristics.

Modernism A movement which started in the early twentieth century. Writers, artists and musicians broke with the conventions of their art forms, producing work that was difficult to understand. It often shocked and disturbed audiences.

Pagan The worship of nature and the seasons.

Pastiche A copy not of a work but of a style or technique, which tries to mimic the original as closely as possible.

Patrilineal Inheritance through the father's line. See also **aristocracy**.

Philology Literally 'the love of words'. Philologists study the ways languages evolve, which often means using literature as evidence of historical changes in languages.

Psalm A song of praise to God. The Psalms form the twentieth Book of the Old Testament of the Holy Bible.

Realism In literature, writing which attempts to simulate peoples' experiences of the world, set in real places and times.

Romanticism An early nineteenth-century movement, which celebrated the beauty of the natural world and peoples' potential for freedom.

FURTHER READING

All the work by Tolkien listed in the Chronology of Major Works is currently available. However, there are several different editions of all the key texts. Readers will have different priorities, and the publishers certainly offer a variety of choices – hardback or paperback, deluxe leatherbound or cheaper clothbound editions. The contents are the same, with one important exception: some of the paperback editions of *The Lord of the Rings* do not include all the appendices. Check before you buy.

Bate, J. and L. Coupe *The Green Studies Reader. From Romanticism to Ecocriticism,* London: Routledge (2000)

Beard, H, and D. Kennedy *Bored of the Rings. The Harvard Lampoon* London: Gollancz (2001)

Bruner, K and J. Ware *Finding God in The Lord of the Rings,* Wheaton, Illinois: Tyndall House (2001)

Campbell, J. *The Hero with a Thousand Faces,* London: Fontana (1993)

Carpenter, H. *J.R.R. Tolkien. A Biography,* London: George Allen and Unwin (1977)

Carpenter, H. (ed.) *The Letters of J.R.R. Tolkien,* London: George Allen and Unwin (1981)

Chance, J. *Tolkien's Art: A Mythology for England* 2nd edition, London: University of Kentucky Press (2001)

Chance, J. *The Lord of the Rings. The Mythology of Power,* London: University of Kentucky Press (2001)

Curry, P. *Defending Middle-Earth,* Edinburgh: Floris (1997)

Gantz, J. (trans.) *The Mabinogion,* London: Penguin (1976)

Heaney, S. (trans.) *Beowulf. A New Translation*, London: Faber (1999)

Isaacs, N, and R. A. Zimbardo, (eds.) *Tolkien and the Critics*, Indiana: University of Notre Dame Press (1968)

Jackson, R. *Fantasy. The Literature of Subversion*, London: Methuen (1981)

Lönnrot, E. *The Kalevala*, K. Bosley (trans.) Oxford: Oxford University Press (1999)

Malory, T. *The Morte d'Arthur*, H. Cooper (ed.) Oxford: Oxford University Press (1998)

Manlove, C. *Modern Fantasy. Five Studies*, Cambridge: Cambridge University Press (1977)

Manlove, C. *The Fantasy Literature of England* London: Macmillan (1999)

Muir, E. 'Strange Epic', *The Observer*, 22/8/1954, p.7

Muir, E. 'The Ring', *The Observer*, 21/11/1954, p.9

Muir, E. 'A Boy's world', *The Observer*, 27/11/1959, p. 11

Shippey, T. *J.R.R. Tolkien: Author of the Century*, London: HarperCollins (2000)

Smiley, J. (trans.) *The Sagas of Icelanders*, London: Penguin (2001)

Swinfen, A. *In Defence of Fantasy*, London: Routledge (1984)

Tolkien, C. *The History of Middle-Earth*, 12 volumes, London: HarperCollins (1983–1996)

Tolkien, J.R.R. (trans.) *Sir Gawain and the Green Knight, Pearl and Sir Orfeo*, London: Allen and Unwin (1975)

INDEX